Dashiell Hammett

Twayne's United States Authors Series

Kenneth Eble, Editor
University of Utah

TUSAS 458

DASHIELL HAMMETT
(1894–1961)
Photograph courtesy of
The Granger Collection

Dashiell Hammett

By William Marling

Case Western Reserve University

Twayne Publishers • *Boston*

Dashiell Hammett

William Marling

Copyright © 1983 by G.K. Hall & Company
All Rights Reserved
Published by Twayne Publishers
A Division of G. K. Hall & Company
70 Lincoln Street
Boston, Massachusetts 02111

Book Production by Marne B. Sultz

Book Design by Barbara Anderson

Printed on permanent/durable acid-free
paper and bound in the United States of
America.

Library of Congress Cataloging in Publication Data

Marling, William, 1951–
Dashiell Hammett.

(Twayne's United States authors series ; TUSAS
458)
Bibliography: p. 135
Includes index.
1. Hammett, Dashiell, 1894–1961
Criticism and interpretation.
I. Title.   II. Series.
PS3515.A4347Z77   1983   813'.52   83-
12600
ISBN 0-8057-7398-3

Contents

About the Author

William Marling was born in Chicago and grew up in the Ohio Valley. He received his B.A. in journalism from the University of Utah, and worked professionally in various parts of the United States for a number of publications, including *Fortune* and *Money*. He earned his Ph.D. from the University of California in 1980. His work on William Carlos Williams has been published in several scholarly journals, and his book *William Carlos Williams and the Painters* appeared in 1982. A published poet and translator, he teaches media writing and American literature at Case Western Reserve University in Cleveland.

Preface

Dashiell Hammett is most commonly known as the author of an exceptional detective novel, *The Maltese Falcon,* which became the paradigm Humphrey Bogart film. Among serious students of the detective genre, however, he has always been much more: the first modern detective to write detective novels, the creator of the "Continental Op," and a founder of the "hard-boiled" school of fiction. But as we are now discovering, Hammett's work has a significant place in major American literature as well.

Hammett's life was varied, controversial, and shadowy. He was a friend of Faulkner, Fitzgerald, and West, as well as the paramour of Lillian Hellman. Some of these people, and many of his experiences as a Pinkerton, he translated into the stuff of his fiction. Exactly what was true and what apocryphal was unclear until Richard Layman's recent biography, *Shadow Man.*

This is the first full-length study of the Hammett corpus to benefit from Layman's work. It is also the first study to explain Hammett's work, from his early pieces in *The Smart Set* through the major novels and even *Tulip,* as a coherent whole. This unity of perspective itself owes to Hammett's instinctual grasp of the way in which American popular fiction from Cooper onward has been able to assume certain chivalric conventions and some of the motifs of the quest, and to deploy them in a contemporary moral framework. This insight on Hammett's work was first advanced in essays by Robert Edenbaum and George Grella. To a lesser extent the framework of this study draws on Steven Marcus's essay on the Op, and on William Ruehlman's study of the American private eye.

In planning this book, I sought to frame a study that would continue to be useful. The five novels and two collections of short stories that have been in mass-market paperback editions since 1972 form the core texts, from which I stray only briefly. These have all the signs of evolving into the canon. I have attempted to let the reader profit from Layman's biography, to which I am indebted, whenever possible. Hammett's life was more important to his work than is usual with an author, and some knowledge of it is pertinent. His dramatic change from Hollywood screenwriter to Communist ideologue is, in particular, a subject that I take up. Thus biography forms the content of my first and last chapters, as well as parts of intermediate chapters. The central chapters focus on Hammett's work. The short stories, though written over fifteen years and numbering over a hundred, are treated in a single chapter that focuses on the best of the anthologized pieces. The first two novels, which were serialized in *Black Mask* magazine (with the attendant disadvantages) are treated in another chapter, which also attempts to rectify the critical mistreatment of *The Dain Curse*. The two major novels—*The Maltese Falcon* and *The Glass Key*—are paired in the fourth chapter. *The Thin Man* is lighter entertainment, typical of Hammett's screenwriting, and therefore in a chapter with his Hollywood work.

My particular thanks to Ellen Dunlap and the staff of the Humanities Research Center, University of Texas–Austin; to Richard Layman, for help at several points; to William Godschalk; to Joyce Martin, my patient typist; and to my editor, Kenneth Eble, whose remarkable qualities as a teacher I tried to keep in mind as I wrote. I owe a debt to Cindy, for her support, and to Robin, who I hope will find this on a library shelf someday, and know where her father was when he should have been playing with her.

William Marling

Case Western Reserve University

Acknowledgments

Grateful acknowledgment is made to Random House Inc. and Alfred A. Knopf, Inc. for permission to print excerpts from *The Big Knockover, The Continental Op, Red Harvest, The Dain Curse, The Maltese Falcon, The Glass Key* and *The Thin Man.*

From *An Unfinished Woman: A Memoir* by Lillian Hellman. © 1969 by Lillian Hellman. Reprinted by permission of Little, Brown and Company.

Excerpts from *Shadow Man: The Life of Dashiell Hammett,* © 1981, by Richard Layman, are reprinted by permission of Harcourt Brace Jovanovich, Inc.

Frontispiece reprinted by permission of The Granger Archive.

Excerpts from the unpublished work of Dashiell Hammett reprinted by permission of the Humanities Research Center, University of Texas at Austin.

Chronology

1894   Samuel Dashiell Hammett born 27 May in St. Mary's County, Maryland.

1909   Quits Baltimore Polytechnic Institute; holds various railroad and industrial jobs.

1915   Becomes a Pinkerton operative.

1918   Joins the U.S. Army. Has first bronchial attack.

1920   Moves to Spokane. Works as Pinkerton again.

1921   Moves to San Francisco. Marries Jose Dolan. Works briefly as Pinkerton. First child born.

1922   First story in the *Smart Set*.

1923   First story featuring the Continental Op, in *Black Mask*. Works steadily at short stories when not ill.

1927   Serial version of *Red Harvest* begins to appear in *Black Mask*.

1929   *Red Harvest* and *The Dain Curse*. Hammett leaves his family, moves to New York City.

1930   *The Maltese Falcon*.

1931   *The Glass Key*. Goes to Hollywood to work for Paramount. Meets Lillian Hellman. Movies scripted by Hammett, or based on his work, begin to appear.

1932   Hammett and Hellman move to the Sutton Club, where Hammett works on *The Thin Man*.

1934   Hammett and Hellman spend time in Florida. *The Thin Man*. March, last short story published by *Collier's*.

1934–1935   MGM releases movie version of *The Thin Man*, and signs Hammett to a contract. Universal buys "On the Make," releases it as *Mister Dynamite*. Paramount releases *The Glass Key*. Warner Brothers releases a version of *The Maltese Falcon*.

1936   Hospitalized for alcoholism.

1937   Involvement in the Loyalist cause in Spanish Civil War, first political activity.

1939   MGM fires Hammett.

1940   Hammett named national chairman of Committee on Election Rights, a group allied with the Communist party.

1941   Third movie version of *The Maltese Falcon,* starring Humphrey Bogart, directed by John Huston, released by Warner Brothers.

1942   Joins the Army at age forty-eight.

1942–1945   Edits the *Adakian,* an army newspaper in the Aleutian Islands.

1946   Returns to New York City; teaches at Jefferson School. Radio serials of his work proliferate. Drinking increases.

1949   Hospitalized again for alcoholism. Takes vow of abstinence.

1950   Returns briefly to Hollywood, is unable to work.

1951   Sent to jail for refusing to testify about Civil Rights Congress bail fund.

1952   On release, Hammett moves to Katonah, New York.

1953   Interrogated by the McCarthy Committee. Abandons "Tulip," his last written work.

1955   Heart attack at Hellman's home on Martha's Vineyard.

1961   Death at Lenox Hill Hospital on 10 January.

Chapter One
Early Life

In the spring of 1931, after he had published *The Maltese Falcon*, Dashiell Hammett threw a party for the people who had helped him when he was a struggling pulp writer in San Francisco. He took a chauffeured limousine up from Los Angeles, checking into a suite at the exclusive Fairmont Hotel. But before the party, he rode downtown to look up Albert Samuels, who had employed him as a copywriter in his lean years, and had loaned him $500 to move East in 1929. After paying back the money, Hammett took him to the party. The revelry lasted a week, and the bills for food and the Prohibition liquor piled up. When it was over, Hammett went back to Samuels and asked for a loan of $800 to cover his debts. Samuels agreeably told Hammett to drop by the next day. When he opened for business, Samuels was greeted by Hammett's black chauffeur, who handed him a note: "Give the jig the bundle. Dashiell Hammett."[1]

The event highlights with rare clarity the central conflict in Dashiell Hammett's life—the theme that gave rise to his best work. Hammett had been, and would always be a child of the streets. Money in the hand was money spent. When he was flush his generosity with money, time, and advice were unstaunchable. But the streets also taught that nothing was permanent: Hammett had a deep-seated mistrust of accumulation, and the most creative part of his life is a chronicle of personal and financial irresponsibility. The only place in which he could reconcile the duty and the distrust was fiction, where he invented a creed of uncommon power for the common man.

Samuel Dashiell Hammett was born on 27 May 1894 on a run-down Maryland farm. His first name was his grandfather's, his middle name his maternal grandmother's maiden name. The De Chiells had been famous in France for their bravery in battle, and Hammett's mother, Annie, who held herself superior to her husband's family, insisted that his name be said with a French emphasis on the second syllable.

If his mother was the source of an aloofness, a sense of pride and honor, his father was an example of frontier profligacy. Richard Hammett was thirty-two when he married Annie Bond, a minister's daughter from Kentucky. A persuasive lover, he convinced her to convert to Catholicism. He called himself a farmer, as his father and grandfather had, but he disliked the labor. He worked briefly as postmaster, a position gained by family influence, and as justice of the peace. Neighbors called Richard a "pure Hammett," meaning that he drank whisky prodigiously, never refused a fight, played a sharp game of poker, and womanized all night. He was a big, handsome man and, as Hammett's biographer points out, "He was stubborn, independent, and his ambition was tempered by a touch of laziness."[2]

His grandfather dominated the chaotic farmhouse in which Dashiell Hammett lived his first six years. After his first wife died, Samuel Biscoe Hammett took a twenty-three-year-old bride, causing a local scandal. They had three children. When Richard and Annie moved in, there were three more. Dashiell had an older sister—Aronica Rebecca, called Reba—and a younger brother named Richard Thomas, known as Dick. Besides cats and dogs and children, the farmhouse was frequented by neighboring Hammetts, card players, and rabbit hunters.

Annie Hammett disapproved of the rough country society, disliked drinking, and considered all Hammett men "undependable." She was known as "Lady" for her insistence on manners and morality, but her frequent illnesses removed her from an arbiter's role. The combination of frequent childbearing, humid air, and cold winters aggravated her tubercular condition. Her health and social ambitions must have been among the reasons the Hammetts moved to Philadelphia in 1900. Hammett remembered little of life in the farmhouse. "The only remarkable thing about my family was that there were, on my mother's side, sixteen army men of France who never saw a battle," he wrote.[3]

In Philadelphia, Richard Hammett took a job as a manufacturer's agent, but salesmanship was not his forte. The next year he moved the family to Baltimore, where he worked first as a streetcar conductor and then as a clerk. The three Hammett children attended Public School No. 72, but made few friends, perhaps because they were not friends themselves. The somewhat temperamental, rather quiet Dashiell was aloof, like his mother; these traits kept his younger brother Richard at a distance. Dashiell seemed competitive, but he had emotional places that he did not allow anyone to touch. Boyhood friend Walter C. Polhaus remembered a hockey game they played: "I was hitting the puck first all the time and it made him very angry. When we were playing the last game, instead of hitting the puck, he hit me with the stick and made a cut over my right eye. When he saw I was bleeding, he got very upset and ran home."[4]

Hammett discovered the West Lexington Library, and brought home armloads of adventures and mysteries. These he read late into the night, which irritated his mother, according to his biographer: "Annie Hammett had one complaint about her son when she visited her friends in Saint Mary's County: he stayed up reading too late at night and she often had to spend an entire morning getting him out of bed."[5] This hungry, eclectic reading became a lifelong habit, of which Lillian Hellman later wrote: "The interests of the day would carry into the nights. . . . It would be impossible for me to remember all that he wanted to learn, but I remember a long year of study on the retina of the eye; how to play chess in your head; the Icelandic sagas; the history of the snapping turtle. . . . The hit or miss reading, the picking up of any book, made for a remarkable mind, neat, accurate, respectful of fact."[6]

Reading must have helped Hammett to qualify for Baltimore Polytechnic Institute, an outstanding public high school in engineering and mechanics, with a reputation for its liberal education; H. L. Mencken was among its graduates. Hammett enrolled in 1908, and history was his best class. But just before his sixteenth birthday his father became seriously ill, and he was forced to quit school. "Dashiell was elected to pick up the pieces," his brother Richard explained. The family business employed Arab fish peddlers, but no amount of enterprise could save it.[7]

The special relationship between Dashiell and his mother intensified when it became his responsibility to provide for the family. Hammett recognized that his mother, though the sole emotional support of the family, was trapped by the petty tyrannies of an ill, vain husband who could not relinquish his Southern gallanthood. Hammett declared often and openly "that he would never treat a woman the way his father treated his mother."[8] Annie Hammett's view of her situation reveals a kind of cold-eyed clarity that became important to her son. If you cannot hold a marriage together with love, she told neighbors, do it with sex. She was too imperious to feel sorry for herself, a trait that Dashiell admired. Later he recalled that she had given him two useful pieces of advice: "Never go out in a boat without oars, and don't waste your time on a woman who can't cook—she's not likely to be any good in the other rooms of the house either."[9]

As the main support of his family, Hammett, then fifteen, was never able to hold a job long. First he worked as a messenger boy for the

Baltimore and Ohio Railroad; later he graduated to freight clerk. When the B & O fired him, he created his first story. He had been late to work every day for a week, he recalled, and finally the boss called him in. He was fired. Hammett gave a nonchalant shrug and turned toward the door. The boss stopped him: "Give me your word it won't happen again, and I'll let you stay on." Hammett paused, shook his head. No, he figured he would be late again. He did not want to have to break his word of honor because of fate. So the boss gave in, and told him to keep the job. But a few weeks later Hammett quit.[10] Like Flitcraft, one of his later fictional totems, Hammett believed in fate, in the overthrow of the present.

He worked sporadically as a stevedore, as a timekeeper and finally as a yardman for another railroad. He described the experiences in a manuscript titled "Seven Pages": "I worked for a while in a freight depot. On my platform were two men who worked together, sweeping out cars, repairing broken crates, sealing doors." One of them, recounted Hammett, "boasted of the hardness of his skull and told stories of butting duels, head-top crashed against head-top until blood came from noses, mouths, ears. His mate had a fly tattooed on his penis."[11]

Next Hammett was a day laborer, working outside in the sun, rain, and snow. Then he got an inside job as a nail machine operator in a box factory. It was all the same; Hammett disliked the routine, the mindless work, the time clocks. Still in his teens, he began to drink casually in corner saloons, and before twenty he initiated himself into the mystery of venereal disease—such was the complexion of love in Hammett's haunts. He began to puzzle and to worry his family and neighbors. He appeared to have few friends, yet he possessed a reserve, a self-assurance born of knockabout survival, of an ability to provide by his wits for a family of five. Some interpreted this aloofness as ambition, others as laziness.

Working for Pinkerton's

Since Hammett never kept a job as long as a year between 1909 and 1915, he was always looking for work. "An enigmatic want-ad took me into the employ of the Pinkerton's National Detective Agency," he wrote, "and I stuck at that until early in 1922."[12] He liked his new social status too, as he later explained in a story:

The fortunes of job-hunting not guided by definite vocational training had taken him into the employ of a private detective agency some ten years ago. He had stayed there, becoming a rather skillful operative, although by disposition not especially fitted for the work, much of which was distasteful to him. But he liked its irregular variety, the assurances of his own cleverness that come frequently to any but the most uniformly successless of detectives, and the occasional full-tilt chase after a fleeing person who was, until a court had decided otherwise, a scoundrel of one sort or another. A detective has a certain prestige in some social divisions, a matter in no way equalized by his lack of standing at all in others, since he usually may either avoid these latter divisions or conceal his profession from them.[13]

The Pinkerton's National Detective Agency was the largest private law enforcement agency in the United States. It was founded in 1850 by Allan Pinkerton, a big, hard-muscled Scot who had served a stint on the Chicago police force. He invented the trademark of his business—the unblinking eye and its motto, "We never sleep," which led to the shorthand tag of "private eye." He was a nonpareil, his business grew, he trained his men well, and his advertising claim was accepted by most people as fact: "No one is as good as a Pinkerton, if it's detective work you're looking for."

The Pinkertons filled a gap between the federal government's small Secret Service and the local police forces. As the nation grew more complex, the gap needed more attention; the Pinkertons were called upon to prevent assassinations, to systematize crime prevention, and to solve difficult cases, especially those crossing many local jurisdictions. Their expertise came to the attention of business leaders and captains of industry. At the turn of the century the movement to organize labor had spread West, following the railroads into mining camps and new industrial areas. The Industrial Workers of the World (I. W. W.) and several smaller radical unions began to organize workers on the basis of their industries, rather than on the basis of their crafts. Industry had learned to deal with craft unions, but when the I. W. W. began to organize the general labor, they called in the Pinkertons. The agency became known for its "union-busting" ability. Pinkertons broke strikes, beat up strikers, burned their headquarters or homes, and safe-guarded the "scabs" who crossed picket lines.

It was a relief to Hammett's family that he joined the Agency; his father had worried that Dashiell's failure to keep a job was turning him into a "communist." The Pinkertons were an antidote for delinquency, as the Marines are supposed to be today. Pinkertons were highly disciplined. They were on twenty-four-hour call, but the basic nature of their work involved extreme quiet: they watched houses for days at a time, they trailed suspects for weeks, they read old files and composed new ones. The agency had that curious discipline of martial organization that also encourages repose. An agent who could not sit quietly to watch or to listen for evidence was fired; one who could not tail a suspect inconspicuously all day was second rate. The starting salary for this work was twenty-one dollars a week in 1915.

By most accounts Dashiell Hammett was a good Pinkerton. "Despite his size—he was 6' 1½" and weighed about 160 at the time—he could follow a suspect all day without being observed," writes his biographer. The assistant manager of the Baltimore office, James Wright, taught Hammett the Pinkerton methods. He was a short, thick-bodied, tough-talking pro whose abilities were famous within the agency.

Hammett learned not only the fundamentals of detection, but also the code of the profession. Wright had an ethos, or professionalism, about his job that was a combination of insight, self-protection, agency policy, and survivor morality. Hammett adopted this approach, seeing that it permitted the detective to do his work well with as little emotional and physical risk as possible. Key to Wright's code were three elements, according to Richard Layman: anonymity, morality, and objectivity:

A good detective must be anonymous, because the less known about him, the less his chances are of having personal information used against him. A good detective neither seeks publicity nor accepts it easily if it comes his way. Accordingly, a Pinkerton operative's reports were anonymous. He was identified by number; one copy of his report was filed at the branch office and another, perhaps abridged or rewritten, was supplied to the client. A Pinkerton was expected to be close-mouthed and secretive about his job. Hammett, for instance, gave his occupation as "clerk" in the city directory while he was a detective in Baltimore. Later, while working as a part-time operative in San Francisco, he described himself as a "broker."[14]

An idealized version of James Wright, who ran the agency in the Continental Building, was to become the model for the Continental Op, and later for Sam Spade. Wright appears to have informed Hammett that morality was personal. The agent's job, bluntly put, was to protect the good people from the bad people. The bad did not live by civil or religious morality. To be bound by those rules in dealing with them was to put oneself at a disadvantage. In Wright's view, a detective might lie, misrepresent, cheat, steal evidence, break promises, blackmail, and emotionally manipulate people in order to bring the criminal to justice. A successful detective ignored the usual rules and conventions. In effect, this was what the client had hired him to do, and he owed the client this service, and the information and results it produced. Wright's loyalty to the client, however, was sometimes superseded by his personal sense of justice, which he dispensed in frontier fashion for crime that might have gone undetected. Nor did he believe in getting caught, either by the police or by his superiors in the agency.

The private detective, notes Layman, had to develop a carefully ordered sense of priorities:

The essential quality which a detective must develop to avoid being consumed by his job is objectivity—an emotional distance from the people with whom he deals. If he becomes emotionally involved with a client, he will forfeit the objectivity required to gather all the available information and observe all the pertinent clues relating to the case. If he allows himself to hate a criminal, he will lose the emotional equilibrium required to protect himself and to make all his decisions coolly and logically.[15]

No record survives of the cases that involved Hammett, because the reports were numerically identified and because a fire destroyed most papers of the Baltimore office.

In and Out of the Army

Hammett quit the Pinkertons to join the Army fifteen months after the United States declared war on Germany. On 12 July 1918 the Army assigned him to the 154th Brigade at Camp Meade, Maryland, only fifteen miles from his home. He trained in the ambulance corps as a driver, but never left the state of Maryland; he spent most of the time fighting the first in a lifelong series of battles with emphysema and tuberculosis.

Soldiers returning home transmitted to the States the Spanish influenza epidemic of 1918. At least 250,000 and possibly 500,000 Americans died of it. Hammett reported to a field hospital on 6 October complaining of the flu. Doctors diagnosed his condition as bronchopneumonia, but after twenty days released him to active duty. He was soon back in the infirmary for acute bronchitis, but stayed only four days. On 29 May 1919 he was back in the hospital with intractable tuberculosis. The doctors decided that he had contracted it in the line of duty, and that he should be declared twenty-five percent disabled and discharged immediately.

The next day Hammett was a civilian. He weighed 140 pounds, had a sore throat, and experienced shortness of breath, dizziness, and coughing.

Tuberculosis had seized him in youth, as it had his mother. Twenty-five years old, Hammett had no choice but to move back to his parents' home. His disability pension amounted to $7.50 a week, not enough to survive on, and although the Pinkertons offered him his old job at $105 a month, he could not work.

Hammett found himself paralyzed by lack of breath when he tried to climb the stairs, nor could he even sit up for more than a few hours before he tired. The dizziness and coughing annoyed, but he also began to hemorrhage. Though he gave up drinking and all but stopped smoking, within a few months Hammett was in the hospital. The doctors reviewed his case and declared him fifty percent disabled, increasing his pension to $50 a month, and advising that he would never be able to work again, let alone as a detective.

Hammett stayed home in bed, an invalid. His older sister Reba was a stenographer, so he was left to his father, with whom he fought, and his brother, who still worked as a clerk. Hammett's tuberculosis was erratic and cyclical; like his mother he had long periods of remission, in which he seemed healthy. During an upturn in his illness, in the spring of 1920, he broke all ties with the family and headed West.

In the West with Pinkerton

In May 1920, Hammett had some money—perhaps he had saved his disability payments. It appears that he set out deliberately to cross the United States to Spokane, Washington, although the damp, cold climate of the Northwest would seem no improvement over the humidity of Baltimore. But there was a Pinkerton agency there. Hammett's health improved; his weight rose to 155, the highest it had been since he entered the Army. He liked detective work, and his assignments took him into Idaho, Utah, and Montana, where the I.W.W. was organizing the miners. It was an area tolerant of idealists, of cast-offs, and the dispossessed. Settlements of Chinese and Irish, who remained after the completion of the transcontinental railroad, flourished among the Mormons and miners. Empires were being built in Virginia City, Butte, and Park City, and the prospect attracted gold seekers and con men. Law enforcement fell to those who wanted to see the law enforced: the great mining concerns hired the Pinkertons.

The spectrum of human motivation and behavior was on display here. Hammett said his most exciting work took place during the Anaconda Copper strike of 1920–1921. The Wobblies (I.W.W.) had been trying to organize these mines for ten years when the company decided to break the union. He told of a strikebreaker named Blackjack Jerome, who drove a flatbed truck down to skid row early in the morning and promised the drunks a hot breakfast and good money for easy work. Then he ran them across the picket lines and dared them to return without his safe escort, which he provided only at the end of a full day of hard work.

Hammett liked to tell the story of a confession won from a prisoner he was transferring from a ranch near Gilt Edge, Montana, to Lewiston, Idaho. It was winter, and Hammett's car broke down in the mountains. He was bundled up in coat, hat, and gloves, but the prisoner wore only the overalls in which he had been captured. As they sat through the long, cold night on the deserted mountain road, the prisoner, who had protested his innocence, grew more and more miserable. At dawn, recounted Hammett, "his morale was so low he made a full confession."[16]

Once, said Hammett, he was sent to arrest a huge railroad track worker named Tony, who was regarded as particularly dangerous with a pick in his hands. The local sheriff dared Hammett to arrest him at work, in front of his fellow "gandy-dancers." Unknown and apparently harmless, Hammett walked into the maintenance yard and called Tony over to the window of the pay shack in a friendly way. Tony dropped his pick and came over; inside Hammett pulled a gun and handcuffed him.

In Oregon Hammett hoped to obtain information about a suspect through a local women's group. He introduced himself as the secretary of the Civic Purity League. No one knew anything, but the leader of the women lectured Hammett, who was smoking, for over an hour on the erotic perils of tobacco for young women. Up near the Canadian border, Hammett worked on the case of the "Midget Bandit." The Pinkertons had convinced the victim of the robbery to brag to the local newspaper about the fate that awaited the robber if he ever showed up again. His pride piqued, the midget returned to give his victim a chance—the Pinkertons were waiting, and arrested him.[17]

Hammett also recalled that he had gone with a group of Pinkertons to arrest a gang of blacks suspected of stealing dynamite. "Everybody thought it was the Germans," he told an interviewer. "When I got inside this house men were being knocked around in fine shape. In the excitement I had a feeling something was wrong, but I could not figure what it was until I happened to look down and saw this negro whittling away at my leg." Lillian Hellman later said that Hammett had "bad cuts on his legs and [an] indentation in his head from being scrappy with criminals."[18]

According to an early Hammett biographer, there were many other such cases:

Hammett ranged the states for Pinkerton: he arrested a smooth talking forger in Pasco, Washington; he rejected an offer to enter the narcotics trade with a pusher in San Diego; he shadowed a man suspected of being an enemy agent in Washington, D.C.; he ran down a window-smasher in Stockton, California; he studied the art of faked prints with Wesley Turner, of the Spokane police bureau; he worked with a stool pigeon to obtain criminal data in Butte, Montana; he tracked down a fugitive swindler in Seattle.[19]

It is impossible to verify most of these stories; some may be purely apocryphal. It is known that the broad education and good times ended in late 1920. Hammett's weight fell to 132 pounds and in November he was admitted to a Public Health Service hospital in Tacoma, Washington. Doctors there considered him 100 percent disabled; he stayed for six and a half months.

Treatment for Tuberculosis

The Cushman Sanatorium, Hammett learned, was a place where rules could be broken without penalty. When his tuberculosis permitted, he joined other patients in playing poker, smuggling liquor into the hospital, and flirting with the nurses. There was a sympathetic head nurse, from whom overnight passes to Seattle were available, and an Alaskan strongman named "Snohomish Whitey" Kaiser, who was particularly interested in the blackjack that Hammett kept among his souvenirs. "Whitey borrowed the blackjack one night and returned it the next morning with ten bucks. Then I read about a man being slugged and robbed of a hundred and eighty dollars on the Puyallup Road the night before. I showed the clip to Whitey, who said people who were robbed always exaggerated the amounts."[20]

Like the other patients, Hammett flirted with the nurses. Jose Nolan, a small delicate woman of twenty-three years, caught his attention. She was from Montana, had a nice smile, and, as an orphan herself, she understood the loneliness of institutions. Hammett struck her as different: proud, handsome, his full head of light brown hair combed in a pompadour. He had dark eyes and a nice smile of his own. He attended to his dress meticulously, even if it was only pajamas. Above all, Jose liked the way that he read all the time and took classes from the vocational instructors.

Hammett asked her for a date—she accepted. Before long he asked the head nurse for additional overnight passes to Seattle: he and Jose went to good restaurants and to the pleasant, green parks. They took a one-room apartment, to have a place to be alone.

The director of the hospital decided, however, that the damp climate was not the best for respiratory patients. He arranged to transfer them to Camp Kearny, outside of San Diego. On 21 February 1921 Hammett took the train south. Camp Kearny was different, however; no booze, no gambling, and few overnight passes. When Hammett did get a pass, he visited the tracks and tourist sights of Tijuana. When he wrote about the period he already imagined himself leaving Jose, whom he named "Evelyn" for the story: "I said: 'Well, goodbye,' and kissed her and went back to my ward. Whitey had stopped snoring and the coyote had stopped barking. Somebody was coughing on the porch facing ours. Except for that and the purr of twenty-some men breathing there was no sound. I smoked a cigarette and thought I was going to miss Evelyn. She wasn't pretty, but she was a lot of fun, a small-bodied girl with a freckled round face that went easily to smiling."

When he recounted their trysts, he imagined them in the desert setting.

We used to leave the hospital around lights out time, walk a little way across the desert, and go down into a small canyon where four trees grouped around a level spot. The night dampness settling on the earth that had cooked all day would turn loose the odor of ground and plants around us. We would lie there until late, looking up through the trees that made maps among the stars, smelling the world and loving and cursing one another. Neither of us ever said anything seriously about loving the other. Our love-making was a thing of rough and tumble athletics and jokes and gay repartee and cursing. She usually stopped her ears in the end because I knew more words.[21]

But Hammett pushed back his doubts when he learned that Jose was pregnant. She quit her job and went home to Anaconda. From there she wrote, he wrote back, and they arranged a marriage.

Perhaps the prospect of a new start aided Hammett's health. By mid-May he entered a long remission, prompting doctors to dismiss him and the Bureau of War Risk Insurance to buy him a train ticket to Seattle. There he took a room, but complained to a local hospital that he was underweight at 135 pounds and that his teeth were abscessed. In June, as if prompted by fate, he moved to San Francisco and rented a room at 120 Ellis Street.

Beginning Again in San Francisco

Hammett was twenty-seven years old, unable to work, with a girlfriend five months pregnant and a disability income of $80 a month. He made a courageous decision when he wrote to Jose to join him; they were married on 7 July 1921 at Saint Mary's Cathedral. Then he turned to the only work in which he had experienced any success. The supervisor of the San Francisco office of the Pinkertons was Phil Geauque; he employed five full time agents, and hired Hammett as a part-timer. In the fall and winter of 1921, working when he could, Hammett was paid on an hourly basis.

But there were other, less tangible compensations. San Francisco was *the* metropolis of the West, the focal point of immigration, mining, industry, export, and such advances in culture as thought up locally or imported from the East. The Volstead Act, which announced Prohibition, was regarded as an incentive to commerce rather than as law. San Francisco became a major port of entry for illegal liquor; speakeasies bought the consent of local authorities out of their stock-in-trade, while networks of rum-runners stretched inland to Butte, Denver, and Phoenix. Houses of prostitution flourished—they were necessary, it was agreed, to preserve the bloom of society's young maidenhood. The Bay area attracted German and Italian immigrants, the latter clustering along the waterfront. An entire Chinese society, complete with criminal gangs, holy men, and a social hierarchy, developed in a twenty square block area downtown.

Government had not really taken hold in San Francisco. "The Hall of Justice was dirty and reeked of evil," recalled columnist Herb Caen of the *San Francisco Chronicle*:

The criminal lawyers were young and hungry and used every shyster trick. . . . The City Hall, the D.A. and the cops ran the town as though they owned it, and they did. Hookers worked upstairs, not on the street; there were hundreds, maybe thousands, most of them named Sally. The two biggest abortion mills—one on Market, the other on Fillmore—were so well known they might as well have had neon signs. You could play roulette in the Marina, roll craps on O'Farrell, play poker on Mason, get rolled at 4 a.m. in a bar on Eddy, and wake up at noon in a Turk Street hotel with a girl whose name you never knew or cared to know. . . . San Francisco was a Sam Spade city.[22]

Hammett was fascinated, excited by a metropolis in which law enforcement was minimal and the opportunities of a private eye so broad. The days he worked were timeless, tense, and vivid; everyone he saw and everything he did accumulated in a fund of experience that he felt he must *do* something with. But it was a brief exposure; according to Layman, "Hammett could not have worked as a San Francisco detective for longer than eight months—half that length of time is more likely."[23]

Jose said that when Hammett was able to do detective work, it took a heavy toll. A suspect he was tailing led Hammett into an alley and pounded his face with a brick; he never forgot to be wary of dark alleys in his stories. Instead of reporting to a hospital, he sat semiconscious at home for two days. For another job Hammett went undercover to the city jail to elicit a confession from a prisoner. He did not get it, but he did carry home an infestation of lice that took a week to clear up. Sometimes shortness of breath pinched him while he shadowed a suspect, forcing him to sit down and to forget the job. But on the basis of this work and that in Spokane, Hammett became an adept at criminal lore.

Four Famous Cases

Though most of his day-to-day work was mundane, Hammett associated himself with four celebrated criminal cases of the era. The Pinkertons were involved in each, but Hammett's connection was probably tangential or concocted on the basis of office gossip. The most famous of these was the Fatty Arbuckle rape case. After an "orgy" in his suite at the prestigious St. Francis Hotel, the 300-pound Arbuckle, a leading comedian and film star, was charged with the death of a would-be actress named Virginia Rappe, whose bladder he purportedly broke with his huge mass in the process of raping her. In fact, as Hammett noted, "The whole thing was a frame-up, arranged by some of the corrupt local newspaper boys. Arbuckle was good copy, so they set him up for a fall."[24]

The heavily covered trial became a circus. The door through which a maid supposedly saw the crime was unhinged and presented in the courtroom. Arbuckle's defense hired the Pinkertons to develop new evidence; Hammett claimed to have been among those operatives assigned: "I sat in the lobby of the Plaza," he wrote in "Seven Pages": "It was the day before the opening of the second absurd attempt to convict Roscoe Arbuckle of something. . . . He looked at me and I at him. I made my gaze as contemptuous as I could. . . . It was amusing. I was working for his attorneys at the time. . . ."[25]

On the basis of new evidence the defense proved that Arbuckle was the victim of an extortion plot; in fact, Virginia Rappe's bladder problem was caused by a long history of venereal disease and a slipshod abortion.

Arbuckle, whom the jury acquitted, had been clowning around drunkenly—on his feet—for the amused Miss Rappe. "The funniest case I ever worked on," commented Hammett: "In trying to convict him, everybody framed everybody else."

Hammett's role in the Nicky Arnstein case is "highly questionable," according to Layman, though it was one of Hammett's favorite anecdotes. Arnstein masterminded the theft of $1.5 million in bonds from a New York brokerage house; when they arrested him, police discovered that he was poised to steal $5 million more. The booking and subsequent trials, one for theft and one for conspiracy to transfer the bonds to Washington, drew national publicity. Hammett liked to tell how he tailed Arnstein to set up the arrest, but the case took place on the East Coast at a time when Hammett was on the West Coast. It is more likely that the anecdote grew from Hammett's friendship in the 1930s with Fanny Brice, the Ziegfeld Follies star who married Arnstein. Hammett used to end the story with the warning, "Don't tell Fanny I did it. She might get mad."[26]

Equally celebrated was the case of Gloomy Gus Shaefer. Gus and his friends robbed a St. Paul, Minnesota, jeweler of $130,000 in silver and gems in December 1921. They fled to Vallejo, near San Francisco, where they holed up in a roadhouse. The Pinkertons were called in, trailed Shaefer to the roadhouse, but held off on his arrest until they could find the loot. Hammett's assignment was to frequent the roadhouse dressed as a wealthy businessman, to see if there was anything for sale. One night he heard Shaefer and his cohorts planning upstairs. He climbed up on a porch roof to listen better, but the roof gave way. Hammett fell and the crooks fled. Subsequently an agent spotted Gloomy Gus and shadowed him to a bank, where he was arrested with the safe deposit box full of loot in his hand.[27]

The dates of all three of these cases conflict with the dates of the final, most curious case in which Hammett alleged his activity. "I was beginning to sour on being a detective," he reported. "The excitement was no longer there, and losing a trip to Australia put the cap on it for me."[28] The foregone trip involved the recovery of $125,000 in English gold sovereigns that were stolen on board the freighter *Sonoma*. The heist occurred at sea between Hawaii and San Francisco; when the boat docked it was sealed off. Police, insurance agents, and Pinkertons swarmed over it, looking for the specie, which they assumed had been stolen by a crew member. The search turned up nothing. The Pinkertons decided to send Hammett back to Australia on the return voyage, hoping that he could find the gold and the thief. "I was delighted," he said. "I'd dreamed of a trip to Australia. It sounded great." But on 29 November, a week before the departure, the Pinkertons made a sweep of the areas they had already searched. According to Hammett, he climbed up a smokestack and looked down in. There was the gold. "I was furious with myself. Why couldn't I have discovered the gold one day out to sea? I'd lost my sea trip. I'd also lost my desire to remain with the Pinkertons."[29]

In fact, the gold was found in the fire hoses and suspended overboard in chests, and was variously credited to two San Francisco detectives, the ship's engineer, and the Pinkertons. The case was solved on 1 December 1921—one day into the Arnstein trial in Washington, and several weeks into the first Arbuckle trial in San Francisco. Hammett's direct involvement is doubtful, but as in the other cases, it was to become the material of his fiction. When he told Lillian Hellman the story years later, the gold was worth $200,000, and he was "a happy man, going free where he had always dreamed of going." As he grew practiced, Hammett made the ending into a personal epiphany. "You haven't sense enough even to be a detective," he said, adding, with a flourish, that he then resigned.[30]

The story is a familiar echo of the earlier anecdote about Hammett and his job as railroad clerk. The impression he left in both cases was that the work had interrupted his destiny. That he had this personal "duty" and that it melded easily with an aggrandizing turn of character revealed a new fictive world, to Hammett, one in which he was whole.

Illness and Poverty

In reality he had suffered another debilitating bout of tuberculosis. By January 1922 his weight had fallen to 126 pounds. According to Layman, "within a month, he was too weak to walk the four blocks to the public library. There were days when he could not get from his bedroom to the bathroom unassisted; he lined the hall of his apartment with chairs so he could rest along the way."[31]

Hammett and his young wife faced grim prospects. She was pregnant and unable to work; after he stopped working, he received only an $80 a month disability pension. Jose managed frugally, buying on credit with the neighborhood butcher and grocer. Hamburger was a big treat, which Hammett himself cooked in his gourmet style, but most meals were meatless. They had no friends, and movies, plays, and restaurants were too expensive.

In October Jose gave birth to a daughter, whom they named Mary Jane Hammett. The doctors told Dashiell that he should limit his contact with the infant to avoid infecting her with tuberculosis. He moved out into the central hall of the three room apartment, where a bed folded down out of the closet. When the baby was four months old, they ran out of money altogether. Dashiell wrote to his father, who sent money and also used the occasion to lecture him.[32]

Toward a Writing Career

The disability pension kept Hammett in contact with the government; when the Veterans Bureau formed, he took advantage of a vocational training program to enter Munson's Business College. There he took classes in stenography and writing, hoping to qualify as a newspaper writer, though soon he decided that he liked advertising better. His weight a mere 135 pounds, Hammett left his bed only four hours a day. He could write and design ads, however, while lying down. He worked on speculation, sending the prepared ad out to a client with his wife or a messenger.

He later reported that his first ad was for his own services. Printed in the *San Francisco Chronicle,* it solicited "any kind of honest work," and listed his previous jobs from warehouseman to detective. "And I can write," it concluded. This advertisement has not been found, but it is known that a San Francisco store traded Hammett a pair of shoes for his second ad. Within a year copywriting became Hammett's bread-and-butter talent.

By the fall of 1922 Hammett was also trying his hand at short stories, and encountering at least some success. He sent his first sketches to the *Smart Set,* which founders H. L. Mencken and George Jean Nathan called "an aristocrat among magazines." The *Smart Set* paid poorly—a penny a word—but attracted a bourgeois readership with its trendy sarcasm. Fitzgerald, Maugham, and Huxley were among its stars, though most of the copy came from unknowns. The class appeal and "serious" intent attracted Hammett, even though he really needed more money. His first piece, "The Parthian Shot," ran 100 words and was published in October 1922. Its central figure, Pauline Key, disliked her obstinate husband and realized that her six-month-old son would be just like him. Just before running away from them, she had the boy christened "Don." The crestfallen reader was left to realize that his name was "Don Key," though he could take satisfaction in Hammett's pay, which was $1.00.

Hammett scored again in the November issue, which contained "The Great Lovers," a discursive survey of twelve exemplars of arrogance. Hammett here appreciated such egomaniacs as Thomas Hart Benton and

Charles IV for those qualities that they shared with him: aloofness, pride, a sense of remove. More interesting than his subject is a newfound ability to control tone and sentence rhythm: "Now that the meek and the humble have inherited the earth and it were arrogance to look down upon any man—the apologetic being the mode in lives—I should like to go monthly to some hidden gallery and, behind drawn curtains, burn perfumed candles."[33]

Hammett began to give the major part of his time and energy to his writing, coming into a sense of his abilities and his future success. "He did not drink excessively," reports Layman, "and he stayed home with his family at night. His worst habit was that he smoked, as he had since he was a teenager—Camels were his brand then, Murads later—despite the warnings from doctors."[34]

When he could visit the library, Hammett boned up on writing. He surveyed the market closely, assessed his background and talents, and set to work. He bought an Underwood portable typewriter, and began to work nightly on the kitchen table. He first penciled notes on a scrap of paper, then wrote a long-hand draft, and finally typed the story for submission. At the end of his first year he had sold twelve pieces to five magazines; none of the stories was longer than a thousand words. They did not bring in much money, and Hammett saw that major success required an area of expertise.

Hammett staked his claim in two pieces that he wrote in 1923. "The Green Elephant," published in the *Smart Set* in October, concerned an apprentice criminal whose accidental possession of $250,000 in stolen money destroyed him. Lacking a compelling plot, this 2,500 word effort—Hammett's longest to date—depended heavily on its ironic tone and psychological penetration of the central character to keep readers interested. That it succeeds is a measure of Hammett's advance. More important, however, was "From the Memoirs of a Private Detective," which consists of twenty-nine paragraphs, each recounting an incident in Hammett's career as a Pinkerton. Some samples:

"I was once falsely accused of perjury and had to perjure myself to escape arrest."

"I was once engaged to discharge a woman's housekeeper."

"I know a forger who left his wife because she had learned to smoke cigarettes while he was serving a term in prison."

"In 1917 in Washington I met a young woman who did not remark that my work must be very interesting."[35]

Hammett was learning to work in a very spare style without sacrificing anything of plot. His handling of irony is unusually sure, yet there is a balancing psychological probity that never slights character. Such talents were not quite suited to the *Smart Set,* and Hammett began to look for better opportunities. Mencken and Nathan may have advised him to focus on the detective market, which they knew from their brief ownership of *Black Mask.* As it turned out, events there would arrange themselves in Dashiell Hammett's favor.

Chapter Two
The Short Stories

The Detective Genre

The detective story is the stepchild of the Gothic novel, a form created by an eclectic Englishman named Horace Walpole. His *Castle of Otranto,* published in 1765, is the foundation of the horror story, although Mary Shelley, wife of the poet, added the scientific aspects in *Frankenstein* (1818).

The idea of detection and figure of the detective were introduced in the nineteenth century by a Frenchman, Francois-Eugène Vidocq. After serving as a soldier, privateer, smuggler, inmate, and secret police spy, Vidocq at age twenty-four could credit himself with a duel for every year of his life. He offered his specialized "security" services to the Paris police, was accepted, and set up his own department, called the Sûreté, which became the basis of modern French intelligence. In a typical year, William Ruehlmann reports, "Vidocq had twelve men working for him, and between them they made 811 arrests, including 15 assassins, 341 thieves and 38 receivers of stolen property."[1]

When Vidocq published his *Memoirs* in 1828, the book was not only popular in France, but received an English translation the same year. In 1833 Vidocq established the first detective agency, Le Bureau des Renseignments, which had the motto "Hatred of rogues! Boundless devotion to trade!" The notoriety of Vidocq's life and work inspired a number of writers. Jean Valjean in Victor Hugo's *Les Misérables* and Balzac's Vautrin in *Le Père Goriot* derived from Vidocq and his exploits. Charles Dickens took detail and character from the *Memoirs* for *Great Expectations*; in America Edgar Allan Poe read and reread Vidocq.

It was Poe who, in five stories between 1840 and 1845, sketched the principles of the detective story. "The unity of effect of impression is a point of the greatest importance," he wrote: "this unity cannot be thoroughly preserved in productions whose perusal cannot be completed in one sitting."[2] Poe's first three "tales" centered on the astounding ability of his sleuth, C. Auguste Dupin. In "Murders in the Rue Morgue," Poe introduced this eccentric, brilliant detective, whose doings were chronicled by an admiring, amiable narrator. Subsequent detectives, including Sherlock Holmes, became more and more eccentric, and Poe's rather uncomprehending narrator turned into Watson and his progeny.

"Rue Morgue" introduced three common detective motifs: the wrongly suspected man, the crime in the sealed room, and the solution by unexpected means. Dupin solved the crime by reading the evidence better than the police, and by noticing clues that they neglected, thus highlighting the importance of inference and observation. In "The Purloined Letter," Poe invented the plot of the stolen document, the recovery of which ensures the safety or security of some important person. Dupin solved this case by two more important formulas: psychological deduction, and evidence in the most obvious place.

In the third Dupin story, "The Mystery of Marie Rogêt," Poe presented the story through newspaper clippings, a technique that attracted Hammett and the literary realists. This story contained no real denouement, because it was a current court case; the reader was left to deduce his own solution—a bold experiment in audience involvement.

Of the other two Poe stories, "Thou Art the Man" is the weaker, but it employs three important techniques: the criminal confesses when faced with the enormity of his crime; the detective follows a trail of false clues; and he deduces that the criminal is the most unlikely person. In "The Gold Bug," which many think Poe's finest mystery, a man finds a cipher promising the discovery of hidden treasure. Every detective writer has tried his hand with this plot, but Hammett's *The Maltese Falcon* is perhaps the best effort.

As a critic, Poe laid down a rationale for the detective story. Unity of tone and a length that permitted reading in a single sitting led Poe to conclude that the mystery was a "tale, a species of composition which admits of the highest development of artistical power in alliance with the widest vigour of imagination." Poe gave three cautions: (1) Failure to preserve the mystery "until the proper moment of denouement, throws all into confusion, so far as regards the *effect* intended." (2) Everything should converge on the denouement: "There should be no word written, of which the tendency, direct or indirect, is not to the one pre-established design." (3) It is imperative that "no undue or inartistic means be employed to conceal the secret of the plot."[3]

By 1870 detective fiction had discovered a wide audience on both sides of the Atlantic. In America Allan Pinkerton followed in Vidocq's path when he published *The Expressman and the Detective* in 1875. Working close to the public pulse, Pinkerton never allowed his protagonist the eccentricity that precluded his immediate perception as a "hero." Pinkerton understood that the public was interested in "the immersion of the eye into an almost surreal under-world, an under-world to which he must adapt in order to get his work done." Pinkerton's prose, as William Ruehlmann notes, "creates an atmosphere of evil commensurate with a sense of the *holiness* of the mission and its necessity for the sanctity of moral order." Pinkerton's second book, *The Molly Maguires and the Detectives* (1877), clarified this theme and sketched the modern American detective: "[The] detective should become, to all intents and purposes, one of the order, and continue so while he remains in the case before us. He should be hardy, tough, and capable of laboring, in season and out of season, to accomplish, unknown to those about him, a single absorbing object."[4]

In England, the detective received a more analytic, stylized treatment, best exemplified by the work of Sir Arthur Conan Doyle. His *Study in Scarlet* (1887) introduced the sturdy Watson and the decayed aesthete Sherlock Holmes. Doyle adopted Poe's formulas, cut the elaborate introductions, restated them in crisp dialogue, and emphasized what Poe touched on lightly—the deduction of great conclusions from trifling clues. He capitalized also on the advances of Wilkie Collins (*The Moonstone*, 1868), whose economy, symmetry, and necessity of plot, are still a model, and he added the use of opium and laudanum by the detective. This made plausible the detective's analytic feats, though verisimilitude has been an endemic problem of the English detective story.

Detective novels boomed in the 1900s. England produced such masters as G. K. Chesterton (*The Innocence of Father Brown*, 1911) and E. C. Bentley (*Trent's Last Case*, 1912). They nearly solved the problem of presenting all the evidence to the reader but mystifying him until the end, as well as the problem of a credible point of view.

Americans, however, sought in popular literature an image of who they thought they were, or wished they were. Some wanted a romantic interest; others demanded an updated myth of the frontier; and some craved that justice the Puritans had sought. American expectations seem particularly to have been conditioned by the Leatherstocking tales of James Fenimore Cooper. A hero of moral virtue, with fantastic visual powers (rather than analytic ones), Natty Bumppo read broken twigs and faint footprints to ferret out evil. Rather than society's rules, he followed a private code. As the frontier moved West, other writers updated Cooper's hero in new locales. That detective fiction took hold in America about 1890, the year picked by historian Frederick Jackson Turner to mark the closing of the frontier, seems auspicious to many scholars. Henry Nash Smith wrote that the hero of the dime cowboy novel became "a self-reliant, two-gun man who behaved in almost exactly the same fashion whether he were outlaw or peace officer. Eventually he was transformed into a detective and ceased in any significant sense to be Western."[5] Leslie Fiedler called the detective a "cowboy adapted to life on the city streets, the embodiment of innocence moving untouched through universal guilt. As created by Dashiell Hammett, he is also the honest proletarian, illuminating the decadent society of the rich."[6]

When Hammett became interested in the detective story in 1923, the genre was experiencing an explosion due to the mass marketing of dime novels. This "Golden Era," as critic John Strachey called it, was the age of A. A. Milne, Agatha Christie, J. S. Fletcher, and Dorothy Sayers. In America, the most popular practitioner was Willard Huntington Wright, who wrote under the pseudonym of S. S. Van Dine about a detective named Philo Vance. The wealthy Wright was also the first editor of the *Smart Set*. The first of his twelve Philo Vance novels was *The Benson Murder Case* (1926). The best-selling Vance was Franklin D. Roosevelt's favorite, and showed the way in which Natty Bumppo and Holmes could be crossbred. Like Hammett's boss, James Wright, Vance always made sure that justice prevailed, even when the law was to the contrary; in *The Bishop Murder Case* (1929) he even engineered a suicide.

The Vance stories appeared in *Scribner's,* one of the respectable "slick paper" magazines, a category including the *Saturday Evening Post, Cosmopolitan,* and *Liberty.* Writers for these periodicals earned up to a dollar a word. At the opposite end of the spectrum were the "pulps," published on cheap newsprint, whose writers toiled for a penny a word. The demand for easily read, popular fiction was immense; over 20,000 magazines were published in 1922. Nearly seventy of these were weekly pulps specializing in romance, flying, Westerns, or detection. An aspiring writer like Hammett could submit to *Detective Stories, Brief Stories,* the *Nick Carter Weekly,* and *Argosy All-Story,* each of which offered readers 150 pages of fiction for ten or fifteen cents. The plots were simple, the characters heroic, the authors plain spoken—it was a mass-produced literature of mass appeal.

When Hammett changed his focus from the *Smart Set* to the pulps in 1923, for reasons that remain unclear, the leading author of the "tough guy" school of pulp detection in the United States was Carroll John Daly. A slight man who had worked as a theater usher and aspired to become an actor, Daly created heroes who said, "I do a little honest shooting once in a while—just in the way of business [but] I never bumped off a guy what didn't need it." In *The Snarl of the Beast,* his hero, Race Williams, added that "right or wrong are not written on the statutes for me, nor do I find my code of morals in the essays of long-winded professors. My ethics are my own." A typical Race Williams story ended on this note: "I sent him crashing through the gates of hell with my bullet in his brain."[7]

The prime vehicle for Daly, and later for Hammett, was *Black Mask,* one of three pulp magazines founded by Mencken and Nathan to fund the *Smart Set.* But they tired in less than a year and sold *Black Mask* to their publishers, who hired George Sutton, Jr., and his associate Harry North in 1922. Seizing on Race Williams, Sutton and North dropped the magazine's earlier interest in Westerns and adventure stories. Under their guidance, the writers of *Black Mask* created standardized, heroic, tough detectives who were willing to disinfect cesspools of crime. "Smashing Detective Stories" read their logo; Hammett was exactly what they sought for the expanding detection market, but Hammett was a bit tired and sick. Only with the rise of editor Joseph T. Shaw, known as "Cap" Shaw, was Hammett induced to return and to produce his classic *Black Mask* stories.

Hammett's Early Short Stories

Hammett's stories rise above the efforts of his fellow *Black Mask* writers because they are framed by Hammett's own almost insupportable tensions. On the one hand, writing afforded him a way of maintaining his aloofness and pride, of identifying and rejecting the inauthenticities he had seen. Working for the Pinkertons, he found most people false, most emotion to be tactical fabrication. The inauthenticity extended, in Hammett's view, to innocent parties, such as Fatty Arbuckle, whom Hammett found guilty on other counts. These other counts are deviations from an ideal character, of which James Wright or Natty Bumppo stand as examples. Hammett's inner duty was to turn up the lie, to speak for the little man.

On the other hand, Hammett, the writer, dealt in the inauthenticities of fiction. Better than most, he could mislead his readers, or suddenly reverse field; under this cloak he remade a world that had not treated him kindly. At the end of a Hammett story, the reality the hero uncovers is no more plausible than the alibi of his suspect. "What happens in Hammett," writes Steven Marcus, "is that what is revealed as 'reality' is a still further fiction-making activity . . . the consciousness present in many of the Op stories and all the novels is that Dashiell Hammett, the writer, is continually doing the same thing as the Op."[8] This consciousness that the process of discovery is a fiction—that the hero's ability to find hidden, latent, and unseen clues in the fictional world gives him superhuman powers—endows Hammett's best work with the external appearance of realism and the internal tensions of the quest or the allegory.

That part of the Hammett hero that puzzles readers, because it is so closely guarded, is the heart of Hammett, at once proud and disengaged yet moved by an unquenchable sense of injustice. Like Jack London and other realists, Hammett in his earliest stories uses an unseen ballast of social concern to mitigate the apparently ruthless or uncouth action of the hero. Hammett began, in fact, with an extraordinary insight into the lives of the office worker, the laborer, the underdog, and the misfit. These first uncollected stories are not detective stories at all.

The narrator of "Nelson Redline" condones his fellow office workers' laziness: "each day's task equalled each other day's task, with no allowance for our becoming more expert with practice, so that toward the end of our term, by carefully concealing our increased proficiency, we had rather an easy time of it." But sympathy never becomes sentiment. This narrator notes, when a co-worker breaks the office code, how the clerks "nurse that momentary speechlessness into deliberate ostracism." When the shunned character flees, the narrator adds, "there was the undeniable fact that all philosophic justification is with him who runs. So, in justice, I couldn't condemn him."[9]

The story "An Inch and a Half of Glory" explores the rise and demise of an office worker whose rescue of a child from a burning building leads him to believe that "desk jobs were well enough for a man who could not rise above them. But nowadays there was a scarcity of—hence there must be a demand for—men whose ancestral courage had not been distilled out of their veins."[10]

Hammett's understanding of the emotions of these working class characters, who were to be his readers, was exceptional. One of his narrators told the audience: "I don't know exactly why I went to his room with him. I knew it was going to be an uncomfortable, even a painful, hour—that he was going to say things that having to listen to would embarrass me. But I went with him to give him an opportunity to explain, to defend himself. My former casual liking for him had, I think, nothing to do with it. That was gone now. I felt sorry for him, in a vague way that made me try to conceal from him my present repugnance." This embarrassment at and aloofness from personal emotion limits Hammett's development in the proletarian direction, and is clearly Hammett's own feeling, as acquaintances have testified. It is also the deep uneasiness from which both his rejection of the unauthentic and his fictionalizing arise. Hammett felt uncertain about emotions; as he remarked when he incarnated them in one unpredictable character, "you don't know approximately what they will do under any given set of circumstances, and so they are sources of uneasiness and confusion. You can't count on them. They make you uncomfortable."[11]

Some of the early stories, such as "The Breech" and "Nelson Redline," have this dis-ease at their thematic centers. Hammett's narrators prefer to be several steps removed, where they may observe the laws of social organization: "Without conventions any sort of group life is impossible, and no division of society is without its canons. The laws of the jungle are not the laws of the drawing room, but they are as certainly existent, and as important to their subjects."[12] It was this interest in the larger social mechanism, in its codes and real functions, that prompted Hammett to read Spencer, Darwin, and later Marx. This "ballast" of social concern is never visible as emotional empathy, but always manifest in a concern for social process.

Hammett tried at first to reveal his detective's emotional life, but the experiment reinforced his decision to remain distant and to employ an objective point of view. In "The Hunter," the ruthless culling of the authentic from the inauthentic holds a personal emotional danger for the detective. It is the problem of means and ends, as Vitt, the detective, simulates moods that he thinks will be of use:

"That's tough." He put into the word and feature all the callousness for which he was fumbling inside. "But the way it stands is that if you're going to fight me on this check business, I'm going to make the going as tough as I can for the pair of you."

Vitt seized the irritation that the idiocy of this reiteration aroused in him, built it up, made a small anger out of it, and his discomfort under the gazes of the woman and child grew less.

A suspicion that all of this was ridiculous came to the detective, but he put it out of his mind. After he got a confession out of his man he could remember things and laugh. Meanwhile, what had to be done to get that confession needed an altogether different mood. If he could achieve some sort of rage. . . .[13]

This simulation makes Vitt merely an actor, and frees him—as is necessary for an allegoric hero—from the personal cost of his actions. But what Vitt does is beat up, arrest, and imprison a penny-ante forger, whose motive is a desire to feed and clothe a widow and her children. Hammett saw the problem, and in the final sentence, after booking the criminal, his Vitt "hastened up to the shopping district. The department stores closed at half past five, and his wife had asked him to bring home three spools of No. 60 black thread." Hammett intended to frame Vitt in a domesticity comparable to his victim's—to show that they were both job-doers, that the impersonal commercial operations of capitalism rolled over both. As he remarked earlier in the story, "A detective is a man employed to do certain defined things: he is not a judge, a god. Every thief has his justification, to hear him tell it."[14] But what the story shows is that a realistic detective, set in a real world, inevitably becomes a hollow man, because the inauthentic that he seeks to destroy, arrest, or remove is inextricably entwined with the authentic, the real, and the emotional. He is as culpable as those he arrests.

The alternative is to make the detective a judge and a god, but to do it covertly. He must be the one who hears the thieves, appraises their justifications, and pursues destruction of the inauthentic while sparing the real. He must not deal with emotions except as falsehoods that ravel the plots he is commissioned to unravel. If he moves on this level, an enormous power comes into his hands, of which the reader is initially ignorant; it is the detective who decides what alibi will be valid, what clue to follow, and, to borrow Robert Champigny's phrase, "what will have happened" at the story's end. In Hammett's work this power is most evident when the detective is drawn taut between world-weary realist and knight in pursuit of the grail.

It took Hammett some time to settle on the move away from emotional intimacy with his characters; at first, in such published stories as "The Sardonic Star of Tom Dooley" and "The Joke on Eloise Morey," he took refuge in heavy irony. But in late 1923, when he wrote "The Second-Story Angel" and "Itchy," his touch lightened. In the second piece Hammett sketched a crook who believed what he read about himself in the newspaper and was captured as a consequence: "Fiction, Itchy knew, meant stories, books. He had never thought of stories as having any connection with actuality, any relation to it. But it seemed they did, and not only with life but with him personally. Books had been written about men like him; that was what the newspapers were getting at."[15] The cavalier manner in which Hammett moves Itchy toward his demise marks his acceptance of the fictional tools at his command.

The Continental Op

The result of Hammett's early work was a detective whom he called, simply, the Continental Op. The Op began as an idealized character. Hammett himself told Frederick Danney that he was modeled on James Wright, his Pinkerton boss in Baltimore. But the Op soon moves in semi-allegoric ways. Much of a reader's appreciation of him rests on an understanding of social code and how Hammett manipulates it to make allegoric gestures. Having grown up with genres like the detective and the western, Americans are not highly conscious of how the cues are manipulated. Because the Op delivers these details objectively, the reader assumes the Op is fair. The reader is thus allowed to be suspicious and to believe himself objective at once, and he assumes that the Op shares his state of mind.

The epitome and chief cause of this effect is Hammett's use of a first-person narrator who purports to be objective. Like a camera eye, the Op only tells what he is seeing; he is never omnipresent, except in the resolutions of stories, and, being nameless, he invites the reader to share his experience. Hammett afflicts the Op with the problems and habits customary to office-workers: back trouble, insomnia, thinning hair and thickening belly. The Op plays cards, gripes about paperwork and complains when the company does not deem Oakland "out of town" for expense account purposes. Details that might forestall complete identification—a wife, bills, politics—are eliminated. Realistic detail and social code screen allegoric structures from the reader's view.

The most obvious of these structures derives from Hammett's understanding that the core of the American detective story, a fascination with death, was also an old topic of allegory. For the reader a good yardstick on this is the Op's changing attitude toward death. Obviously he cannot die, but in the earlier stories Hammett brought him to the edge of death frequently; it was a good way to bare the Op's soul, to elicit reader sympathy. Later the Op's brushes with death became rude gestures at fate, and he succumbed eventually, not to death, but to world-weariness. William Ruehlman calls him a "saint with a gun" and places him in the tradition of James Fenimore Cooper's frontier romances. John Cawelti, another critic, calls him a "traditional man of virtue in an amoral and corrupt world," forced to "take over the basic moral functions of exposure, protection, judgment and execution." But as the following section will show, the Op's code is blurry, if not cynical, when he reaches full development. More to the point is Angus Fletcher's comment that such a semi-allegoric figure stands "part way between the human and the divine spheres," and can "act free of the usual moral restraints, even when he is acting morally, since he is moral only in the interests of his power over other men."

The fascination with death is evident even in the earliest stories. In "The Tenth Clew" the Op is blackjacked and believes he is dying when his attackers dump him in San Francisco Bay.

Weariness settled upon me, and a sense of futility. The water was no longer cold. I was warm with a comfortable, soothing numbness. My head stopped throbbing; there was no feeling at all in it now. No lights, now, but the sound of fog-horns . . . fog-horns . . . fog-horns ahead of me, behind me, to either side, annoying me, irritating me.[16]

Hold off, Charon—the Op rouses himself. Life is valuable for the Op yet, as it is in "The House in Turk St." when he overhears the inscrutable Tai vetoing his execution: "My gratitude went out to the British voice! Somebody was in favor, at least to the extent of letting me live. I hadn't been very cheerful these last few minutes." But this same story, slightly later, shows a more cautious Op: "I might have stalked my enemies through the dark house, and possibly have nabbed them; but most likely I would simply have succeeded in getting myself shot. And I don't like to be shot." (CO, 99, 111)

After this story and its sequel, "The Girl with the Silver Eyes," the Op never puts himself deliberately in the path of danger. This heightens the implicit fear of death, or the fear of what death will reveal.

Only a year later, in "The Golden Horseshoe," the Op is no longer "a young sprout of twenty or so, newly attached to the Continental Detective Agency." Instead, he says, "the fifteen years that had slid by since then had dulled my appetite for rough stuff." This story and "The Whosis Kid" (March 1925) mark the maturation of the Op's career. Emphatically a working stiff, he suffers for the drinking bouts he initiates in the first story, and makes sure that he gets his "three square" a day in the second.

The Op's dehumanization by his work coincides with the rise of his "god-like" powers. In "The Golden Horseshoe," his ends—the necessity of success—have begun to corrupt his means. Much of the story's impact owes to the violence done the reader's sense of justice by the suggestion that God isn't fair. In "The Whosis Kid" Hammett reveals the Op as calculating:

For myself I counted on coming through all in one piece. Few men *get* killed. Most of those who meet sudden ends *get themselves* killed. I've had twenty years of experience at dodging that. I can count on being one of the survivors of whatever blow-up there is. And I hope to take most of the other survivors for a ride. (*CO,* 218)

The Op's explanation is really an assurance that he is immortal, since the great unstated condition is death.

In "The Scorched Face" (May 1925) the Op exercises any means at his disposal. He invades the privacy of Mr. Correll, whose wife committed suicide. When Correll objects, the Op thinks: "That was silly. I felt sorry for this young man whose wife had killed herself. Apart from that, I had work to do. I tightened the screws." A few lines later the Op threatens to "advertise" her suicide in the newspapers. The Op's obvious use of immoral powers in the name of morality, is increasingly displaced on his boss, the Old Man "with his gentle eyes behind gold spectacles and his mild smile, hiding the fact that fifty years of sleuthing had left him without any feelings at all on any subject."[17]

In "The Big Knockover" and "$106,000 Blood Money," the Op's use of immoral means for moral ends succeeds only because Hammett makes him exceptionally empathetic. "I was no fire-haired young rowdy," he says. "I was pushing forty, and I was twenty pounds overweight. I had the liking for ease that goes with that age and weight." He no longer does any spadework; he merely judges the guilty at the right time. He tells readers he is an organization man "settled down to cigarettes, guesses on who'd be the next heavyweight champion and where to get good gin." (*BK,* 388, 399, 381), but he is headed for the same dehumanization that characterizes his boss.

Fifty years of crook-hunting for the Continental had emptied him of everything except brains and a softspoken shell of politeness that was the same whether things went good or bad—and meant as little at one time as another. We who worked under him were proud of his cold-bloodedness. We used to boast that he could spit icicles in July, and we called him Pontius Pilate among ourselves, because he smiled politely when he sent us out to be crucified on suicidal jobs. (*BK,* 359)

The Op of "The Tenth Clew" is gone. It is no mystery that after "$106,000 Blood Money," the Op says, "I'm going to take a couple of weeks off," but never returns.

Classical Formulas in the Op Stories

Hammett wrote the first widely anthologized Op story, "The Tenth Clew," in late 1923. In style and plot this story marks a new level of accomplishment. The first part of it concerns nine clues, some plausible, most preposterous, that seem to link the murder of Leopold Gantvoort to a vengeful Frenchman, Emil Bonfils. But the clues prove contradictory: Hammett is employing one of Poe's classic formulas—the trail of false clues laid down by the murderer. Finally the Op, and his police colleague Sergeant O'Gar, discover the tenth clue, which is that the first nine are false. They decide that the mystery rests with old Gantvoort's girl friend, Creda Dexter. Judging from her beauty, the Op infers a romantic triangle. He breaks the case by confronting her "brother" Madden, who, with an accomplice, blackjacks and dumps the Op into San Francisco Bay. But the Op revives in time to nab the pair with Sergeant O'Gar. The crime is pinned to Madden, who adopts an Iago-like silence, but his "sister" Creda confesses for him, providing the denouement and making her professed innocence and genuine love for old Gantvoort more credible. The interesting use of the classic "false trail" is not well carried out; Madden's purpose in setting out the misleading clues and in telephoning the Op are unexplained. Also left rough is the Op's comment at the end: "I don't believe her [Creda's] enjoyment of her three-quarters of a million dollars is spoiled a bit by any qualms over what she did to Madden." The facts set out earlier clearly make young Gantvoort the heir. Despite the loose ends, "The Tenth Clew" shows the hand of a confident stylist: every word is in a chosen place. There is more rapidity of pace and consistency of characterization than Hammett had yet been able to attain.

The classic formulas also appear in "The Gatewood Caper" (October 1923), a less satisfying story in which the central enigma is a variant of the "sealed room" problem. When millionaire Harvey Gatewood's daughter is "kidnapped," the Op and Sergeant O'Gar advise him to pay the ransom, so they may find, follow, and arrest the criminal. He does, but they do not; the "kidnapper" vanishes into an alley with no apparent egress. As customary, there is an unexpected "means." The criminal has rented an apartment on the alley, and "vanished" by locking the back door to his building behind him, then exiting through the front door.

Hammett returned to the sealed room problem seven years later in "The Farewell Murder," another middling story. The problem here is how Karalov, who hires the Op, could be killed by Sherry, whom the Op is certain was at the time on a train to Los Angeles—a suspect in a locked room, in other words. The answer is that Sherry did not do it; Karalov's apparent friend Rringo did it. Hammett does not play fairly with the reader, however, since at the time of the murder he portrays Rringo as suffering a disabling injury.

The classic problems were not Hammett's strength, nor the chief interest of his editors at *Black Mask,* but he did pay homage to them again in an exceptional later story, "Fly Paper." The Op calls this search for runaway Sue Hambleton "a wandering daughter job." Before he can find her, she is poisoned, which causes the other principals to kill each other. When the Op investigates the deaths, he finds a copy of *The Count of Monte Cristo* wrapped in flypaper behind a refrigerator. "Ah, the arsenical fly paper, the Maybrick-Seddons trick," exclaims his boss. But the sequence and motive for the murders remain unclear until the Old Man remembers a passage in the novel that explains the mechanics and psychology of slow poisoning. Though both the logic and resolution of "Fly Paper" come from *The Count of Monte Cristo,* the homage is a graceful close to an excellent story.

Hammett's early investigation of the classic formulae turned up no impelling material, however; the formulas were not adaptable to a Natty Bumppo readership. They emphasized foiling the reader and astonishing him with witty resolutions. Hammett preferred, and saw that his audience required, strong plotting and vivid characterization in an intensely physical world.

Thus "The House in Turk Street," published in the spring of 1924, adds a detailed foreground and a "romantic interest" to achieve its complexity. While inquiring after a runaway, the Op meets the elderly Mr. and Mrs. Quarre, who invite him in for tea and cookies. Shortly afterward, an ugly con named Hook puts a gun to the surprised detective's head: he foolishly reveals to the Op that the Quarres are a front for a bond-heist involving himself, an English-educated Chinese named Tai, and a beautiful woman with grey eyes named Elvira. The Op has stumbled on their hide-out. They bind and gag him and prepare to leave; the Op is entirely the bystander in a plot that develops through the misapprehended meaning of his appearance.

Then Elvira, who has seduced Hook, decides to use the confusion as a cover to steal the bonds. She appeals to Hook to kill Tai. He tries and fails, but Elvira hides the bonds during the tussle. Only the Op sees, which establishes a link between the two of them: "her eyes twinkled with a flash of mirth as they met mine," he reports. (*CO*, 106) After the gang departs, the Op escapes with Tai's aid, and kills Hook when the latter returns. Then he hides the bonds in a new place, waiting for Tai and Elvira to return and interrogate him. They do, leading Hammett to discover one of his best stock situations—the "apartment drama" with a central female character—and one of his best themes: that greed divides the crooks and makes possible their capture.

When Elvira finds the Op, "her eyes snap scornfully." When Tai finds them both, he offers to "give her" to the Op, though he loves her. The scene in the apartment is a tense three-cornered stand-off. For the first time in any Hammett story, events turn on a woman who is both criminal and attractive. In the gunplay that follows, initiated when the disgruntled Quarres return and Tai kills them, Elvira escapes. Only Tai is left alive to hear the Op explain ironically that he "was trying to find a young fellow named Fisher who left his Tacoma home in anger a week or two ago" (*CO*, 117). The resolution unfolds more promising material than the story's development contained. Besides the ironic ending, the sketch of "Tai Choon Tau . . . the brains of the mob" anticipates the later Chang Li Ching and a legion of Fu Manchu bad-guys after him.

Hammett recognized that the crooks divided among themselves in the claustrophobic confines of an apartment offered a potent dramatic situation. It placed the treacherous face to face, heightened tension by reducing movement, and by joining constriction and violence, offered a metaphor for modern life. Introduced to such a locale, the characters need only be left to work out their fates.

Hammett tried it again in "The Whosis Kid" a bit later. Hunting the character of the title, the Op incidentally rescues Inés Almad, a dark foreign siren. He accompanies her home, and in her apartment meets the Kid and Edouard Maurois, who have come to divide with Inés the loot from a robbery. Since crooks never share in Hammett's stories, a stand-off and violence ensue. The resolution is neither as tidy nor as ironic as in "The House in Turk St.," but many of the details—Inés is threatened with a strip-search, the mastermind is an oily foreigner—will appear in *The Maltese Falcon*. What could animate "The Whosis Kid" but does not is the relation between the Op and the principal female character. Inés, like Elvira, is a femme fatale, but neither the Op nor his creator have clarified the degree to which the detective is vulnerable.

Hammett addressed that material in a sequel to "The House in Turk Street" involving Elvira. "The Girl with the Silver Eyes" was published in the *Black Mask* in June 1924. In this story Elvira changes her name to Jeanne Delano. The poet Burke Pangburn thinks her the most beautiful woman in the world. She wins Pangburn by praising his poetry, convinces him to forge a check on his rich brother-in-law for $20,000, and then disappears. The Op thinks the case suspicious; at first he declines it out of regard for his agency's reputation. "I am only a hired man and have to go by the rules," he says. When the Continental Agency takes the case, he proceeds in a methodical, realistic manner. He goes to banks; he compares checks and signatures; he traces baggage tickets and transfers; he checks weather reports and prevails on clerks at taxi companies to search their log-books. These days of work he condenses into one paragraph when he gives an update to the Old Man.

When Delano and Pangburn are seen together at a roadhouse of larcenous repute, the Op deploys one of his informants. In Porky Grout— "a liar . . . a thief . . . a hophead"—Hammett portrays the marginal type nakedly. The trick is "keeping him under my heel," notes the Op. While Grout stakes out the roadhouse, the Op meticulously tracks down more leads. Someone in Baltimore has mailed Pangburn letters from Delano, someone else taxied between her abandoned apartment and the Marquis Hotel. The Op sweet-talks telephone operators to learn more, and then dispatches Dick Foley, one of the most extraordinary minor characters in the Hammett opus, to tail the suspect: " 'Damnedest!' The little Canadian talks like a telegram when his peace of mind is disturbed, and just now he was decidedly peevish. 'Took me two blocks. Shook me. Only taxi in sight' " (*CO*, 152). The appearance of Foley underlines the increasing complexity of Hammett's code. Communication in the most objective manner possible is now an implicit yardstick of character for the Op, as well as the form of Hammett's narrative. Immediately after Foley, loud-mouthed Porky Grout appears, boasting to the Op, "I knocked it over for you, kid!"

The shoot-out, car chase, and confrontation that follow on the Op's reconnaissance of the roadhouse constitute an exceptional passage in Hammett's work. Watching Jeanne Delano the Op notices "a mocking smile that bared the edges of razor-sharp little animal-teeth. And with the smile I knew her!" This detail of physiognomy will typify most of Hammett's later femme fatales, and tells that his interest has shifted. Burke Pangburn and his brother-in-law fade. "This is the idea," announces the Op, as he bursts into the room, "I want the girl for a murder a couple of months back" (*CO,* 160). The lights go out and they fight; the change in pace is prose adrenalin. Footwork and preparation so methodical that they seem to be ritual purification lead to pure action, which is given its sanctity by emerging allegoric relationships. Not Burke, not the forgery, not the gunplay but the Op's quest for Jeanne is what counts. Can he withstand her allure? Burke is dead by this point. Tai is dead. Porky Grout dies defending Jeanne from the Op. She flees. But the detective has a huge, powerful car at his disposal. He overtakes Jeanne and Fag Kilcourse. Kilcourse dies. It is Jeanne and Everyman.

"She was a thing to start crazy thoughts even in the head of an unimaginative middle-aged thief catcher," says the Op. "She looked at me with a gaze that I couldn't fathom. . . . I was uncomfortable along the spine" (*CO,* 167). All manner of thrust and parry between the sexes follows, the Op adopting the role of gallant, Jeanne that of damsel. They stop along the roadside. Jeanne attempts his seduction:

> If you were to take me in your arms and hold me close to the chest that I am already leaning against, and if you were to tell me that there is no jail ahead for me just now, I would be glad of course. But, though for a while you might hold me, you would be only one of the men with which I am familiar: men who love and are used and are succeeded by other men. But because you do none of these things, because you are a wooden block of a man, I find myself wanting you. Would I tell you this, little fat detective, if I were playing a game? (*CO,* 175)

After several minutes, the Op comes to his limit. "You're beautiful as all hell!" he shouts, and flings her against the door. He remembers Porky Grout and the other dead; only the Op's quest sets him above them. He can resist Jeanne because once she paints his fate allegorically, his code sanctions any action that preserves the quest. Hammett attended to strictly realistic interpretations as well: Jeanne has said a few pages earlier that "everyone in the world is either a fellow crook or a prospective victim." The twin detailing of his decision makes the reader forget that the Op is really "a judge and a god."

When he somewhat uncertainly turns Jeanne in, she "put her mouth close to my ear so that her breath was warm again on my cheek, as it had been in the car, and whispered the vilest epithet of which the English language is capable," says the Op. End of story—a tour de force of plot and characterization, but also a discovery for Hammett of the depth and potency of archetypes.

When he returned to the theme eighteen months later, in "The Gutting of Couffignal," Hammett made more explicit the danger posed by the femme fatale and the Op's proper response. Princess Zhukovski offers her body. "You think I'm a man and you're a woman. That's wrong," the Op responds, "I'm a man-hunter and you're something that's been running in front of me. There's nothing human about it." (*BK*, 34)

The Op in Adventure Stories

In 1924 Hammett wrote the first in a series of stories that beckoned to the "adventure" readership. "The Golden Horseshoe" takes place in Tijuana; it was followed the next year by "Corkscrew," a detective Western set in Arizona; by "Ber-Bulu," in the Philippines; by "Dead Yellow Women," in Chinatown; and eventually by the Balkan intrigue of "This King Business."

"The Golden Horseshoe" is an average piece of plotting and detection, but it is important for the development of the Op's character and for its stunning conclusion, which rests on the Op's willingness to falsify evidence. Initially the story concerns Norman Ashcraft, a missing architect whose wife wants him back. Ashcraft cannot decide whether to return and commits suicide (he will be reincarnated as the character Flitcraft in *The Maltese Falcon*). When he dies, Ashcraft's identity is assumed by a hotel-burglar named Ed Bohannon, who finds Mrs. Ashcraft willing to send him generous amounts of money in exchange for vague promises that he will return.

The Op is called in to determine the whereabouts of "Ashcraft" and the likelihood of his return—nothing exciting, but the Op, to whom Hammett adds paunch and years, is slightly weary anyway. He stakes out the post office, first intimidating and then jailing an accomplice of Ashcraft in order to get his address. It is the "Golden Horseshoe Cafe" in Tijuana. Hammett sketches the scene of "dirty side streets taking care of the dives that couldn't find room on the main street" with great fidelity.

He finds Ashcraft easily, and engages him in a three-day drinking contest. The rivalry works toward Hammett's central insight into the underworld: universal greed leads to universal mistrust. "Ashcraft and I were as thick as thieves, on the surface, but neither of us ever lost his distrust of the other, no matter how drunk we got" (*CO*, 62). When the binge ends, the Op returns to San Francisco, where he finds Mrs. Ashcraft and her two servants dead. He suspects Bohannon as the mastermind and returns to Tijuana to see if he can discover an accomplice. He settles on the bar's bouncer, a "tall, skinny man with a long yellow neck" named Gooseneck Flinn. The Op hires four men to enter the bar and identify Flinn, and when they do Flinn panics. The Op wants the same from Bohannon and his girl friend, but Flinn and the girl kill each other. After an auto chase and a foot race, complete with arroyo shoot-out, the Op captures Bohannon, who explains how he hid in a closet during the real Ashcraft's suicide. But he declines to state that he arranged Mrs. Ashcraft's murder. When the Op asks him to pick up the nearer of two cigarettes if he "did a certain thing," however, Bohannon reveals his complicity. Both know this is inadmissible in court. Satisfied that Bohannon is responsible for the deaths, the Op administers justice:

"I can't put you up for the murders you engineered in San Francisco; but I can sock you with the one you didn't do in Seattle—so justice won't be cheated. You're going to Seattle, Ed, to hang for Ashcraft's suicide."
    And he did. (CO, 90)

The unfortunate Bohannon set himself up for the ironic ending by destroying a suicide note that Ashcraft left; the Op's sentence seems immediately appropriate because it implies a causal relationship linking past and present, but a rereading shows that the Op has made a simple subjective evaluation of character. Hammett developed this ending earlier, in "The Joke on Eloise Morey," and pressed the appeal of biblical vengeance under the guise of impartial justice again in other stories.

The reverse side of this "justice" is shown in "The Scorched Face," published in *Black Mask* in May 1925. Myra and Ruth Banbrock are missing, another "wandering daughter case" (like "Fly Paper," "$106,000 Blood Money," and "The Gatewood Caper"). The Op is unable to learn much, until Mrs. Stuart Correll, one of the girls' friends, commits suicide after interrogation. A difference in the testimonies of Mrs. Correll and the Banbrocks give the Op his first lead, but it goes nowhere.

Then Hammett introduces Pat Reddy, "a big blond Irishman who went in for the spectacular in his lazy way." Reddy's absolute sense of justice once led him to arrest, and later to marry, the daughter of a wealthy coffee-importer. But he "kept on working," notes an approving Op; "I don't know what his wife did with her money, but . . . there was no difference in him . . ." (BK, 85). The only favorable portrait of the rich in the Hammett opus, Reddy plays Chingachgook to the Op's Natty

Bumppo. Their case is becalmed until an up-country grape grower discovers a charred photograph that he recognizes from the newspapers. The Op and a deputy stalk through the woods, the Op admitting "I'm a shine Indian." They find Ruth Banbrock: "At the base of a tree, on her side, her knees drawn up close to her body, a girl was dead. She wasn't nice to see. Birds had been at her" (*BK, 89*).

But the leads go nowhere. The Op resorts to basic detective work; he makes lists of all of those who have committed suicide recently and he interviews their relatives. He discovers that many of them knew Raymond Elwood, a sleek young real estate agent. Dick Foley, by now a regular supporting actor, tails Elwood, discovering that he spends afternoons with various wealthy women in a yellow house on Telegraph Hill.

The case breaks when Myra appears at the house. Rephrasing one of Poe's maxims, the Op notes that "The crazier the people you are sleuthing act, as a rule, the nearer you are to an ending of your troubles" (*BK, 99*). Deciding that his policeman friend can get the necessary papers "fixed up afterward," the Op persuades Reddy to break into the house. They find "a small room packed and tangled with bodies. Live bodies, seething, writhing. The room was a funnel into which men and women had been poured. . . . Some had no clothes" (*BK, 102*).

Several people are killed, including Raymond Elwood and his corps of burly black servants, before the Op finds a photography darkroom and a safe in the basement. There too is Myra, smoking gun in hand. She has killed Hador, the mastermind of the extortion ring, a "queer little man" who dressed in "black velvet blouse and breeches, black silk stockings and skull cap, black patent leather pumps. His face was small and old and bony but smooth as stone, without line or wrinkle" (*BK, 107*). Everything but cloven feet.

"Hador was a devil," explains Myra; "He told you things and you believed them. You couldn't help it." This exculpation prepares Pat Reddy, the only one accountable to the law, for a rationale that will cover up Myra's crime. The Op points out that two women have committed suicide rather than admit to the orgies. How many more will try when the news of Hador's death leaks out? The Op constructs an alternate version, in which Reddy shoots Hador. He wins Reddy's assent, but the policeman is reluctant when the Op proposes to destroy all the evidence: "They're photographs of people, Pat, mostly women and girls, and some of them are pretty rotten." But most of them are rich. And though the Op eventually wins Reddy to his notion of the greater common good, the Op is simply protecting his client for her rich father. Reddy is the only standardbearer of justice in the story; the Op is a hired man of the rich. Lest a reader ponder this too deeply, Hammett adds a twist, as in "The Golden Horseshoe." Here, though, he makes the Op the benefactor of the unwitting Reddy: "The sixth photograph in the stack," notes the Op at the end, "had been of his wife—the coffee-importer's reckless hot-eyed daughter" (BK, 115).

"The Scorched Face," viewed objectively, shows that the rich escape justice. Hammett invites the reader to think that justice is done because the essentially innocent are protected; but in fact Myra has murdered Hador. Codes begin to bend as Hammett discovers the Op's entrancing power to create alternate realities. The rich are sympathetic only through Reddy, but his principal characteristic is that he has not changed—he acts poor, and could not be further from the adventurism of the rich. A cynicism about wealth, born of his reading, begins to tint Hammett's work.

"Dead Yellow Women"

"Dead Yellow Women" is one of the best stories Hammett ever wrote. He set this long, 20,000 word piece (*Black Mask,* November 1925) in San Francisco's Chinatown, and the place has hardly had a rest in detective fiction since. The plot turns on the collaboration of Lillian Shan, a severely beautiful Chinese-American woman, with Chang Li Ching, the feudal lord of Chinatown. Unknown to the Op, whom Miss Shan hires to investigate two murders at her seafront mansion, Shan and Ching run guns to the anti-Japanese forces of Sun-yat-sen. Shan's mansion is the debarkation point, but the murders do not figure in.

The Op penetrates Chang Li Ching's circle through two informers, a Filipino boy called Cipriano and a career con named Dummy Uhl. Like Porky Grout, Uhl proves untrustworthy, so the Op arranges for his informer to shoot him with blanks, then has Dick Foley tail Uhl when he flees. Foley makes one of his best cameo appearances:

"Good pickings!" he said when he came in. The little Canadian talks like a thrifty man's telegram. "Beat it for phone. Called Hotel Irvington. Booth— couldn't get anything but number. Ought to be enough. Then Chinatown. Dived in cellar west side Waverly Place. Couldn't stick close enough to spot place. Afraid to take chance hanging around. How do you like it?" (BK, 204)

The quarry is a con called the Whistler; in the Continental files the Op finds a picture of him, wearing a Japanese war medal as he bilks Japanese immigrants of their money, and he puts the photo in his pocket. All leads converge on Chinatown, which becomes a microcosm of the inscrutability and hostility of a larger world. But the Op is reduced to sitting on the doorstep of Chang Li Ching, his idealized foe ("my idea of a man worth working against," says the Op). To find him the Op must run a maze, with a Chinese guide. This passage echoes grail motifs so closely that, when the Op engages Ching on his own terms, which are wordplay, the unexpected levity surprises the reader: it suggests that verbal play is the core of the quest. Ching addresses the Op: "If the Terror of Evildoers will honor one of my deplorable chairs by resting his divine body on it, I can assure him the chair shall be burned afterward, so no lesser being may use it. Or will the Prince of Thief-catchers permit me to send a servant to his palace for a chair worthy of him?" The Op decides to play: "'It's only because I'm weak-kneed with awe of the mighty Chang Li Ching that I dare to sit down,' I explained" (*BK*, 212).

The interview produces no leads. The case cracks when Dick Foley, shadowing the Whistler, seizes on the bootlegging activities of Lillian Shan's boy friend Jack Garthorne, who says that the Whistler runs illegal immigrants and liquor into the country and only a few guns out. Garthorne's role is to romance Shan away from the scene.

When the Op returns to converse with Chang Li Ching, he finds Garthorne, a "slavey" girl, and then Lillian Shan dressed as a Mongolian queen—"come back to her people," she explains. The Op tells how the Whistler has duped her.

They confront Ching and the Whistler in another part of the labyrinth. To avoid verbal gymnastics, the Op gives Ching the "photograph of The Whistler standing in a group of Japs, the medal of the Order of the Rising Sun on his chest." When the Op next looks, the Whistler is "slumped down in an attitude of defeat," killed by mysterious means. The rest of the story's principals go free; justice is served when Ching gives seven of the Whistler's men to the police. Hammett ends the story with a bad joke about Chinese restaurants and a note from Ching alluding in flowery language to the fact that he has discovered the Op's means of solving the case.

Except for a few racist overtones (Hammett's repeated references to "the smell of unwashed Chinese"), the story is told from a sustained distance. The Op rarely drops his irony and detachment, which reinforces the effect of the hyperbolic conversations and distracts the reader from the quest motifs. The solution to the quest lies at the end of labyrinths and mazes; not only are these actual blind alleys in Chinatown, but figurative ones, such as Lillian Shan's research into "old cabalistic manuscripts." The solution to the quest turns out to be a facsimile of reality adroitly manipulated by the Op: the "real" but false photo of the Whistler. This fools even Ching, whose final note expresses his resolve to "not again ever place his feeble wits in opposition to the *irresistible will* and dazzling intellect" of the Op (*BK,* 249; my italics). The irony grows when the reader realizes that the note is a compliment, paid by one of his finest creations, to the author, who points to his own "irresistible will" in planning and executing the plot that lead on Ching and the reader.

Like "Dead Yellow Women," "The Gutting of Couffignal" (December 1925) is an attempt to find a usable, exotic locale near San Francisco. An example of Hammett's style at its smoothest, this story is organized on the scale of war rather than on that of private detection. Both stories intend to paint broad canvases, for Hammett was training for longer work. In "Couffignal" he hoped to sustain a long narrative drive, but got bogged down in unexplained details. He returned to a manageable scale in his two notable efforts of 1926, "The Nails in Mr. Caterer" and "The Creeping Siamese," the latter attempting to exploit the Chinese theme again, but with mixed results. Then Hammett's work tailed off a bit.

The decline may have been due to domestic factors. Jose became pregnant again, and Hammett decided to look for substantial, remunerative work. He put an ad in the *San Francisco Chronicle,* and Albert Samuels, owner of the oldest jewelry chain in the city, hired him as advertising manager for $350 a month. Samuels allowed Hammett, of whom he grew fond, to break many of his office prohibitions: there was an affair with a secretary and on-the-job intoxication. The Baltimore Dashiell Hammett, the street gamin who was goofing off to ease the tension at home, reasserted himself. There was no showdown, however, because Hammett collapsed at work on 20 July 1926, hemorrhaging from the lungs and, medical tests showed, suffering from hepatitis as well as tuberculosis.[18]

Toward Longer Works

It was eleven months before another short story appeared, but when it did Hammett showed that his eye was on longer, more profitable work.

"The Big Knockover" (February 1927) and its sequel "$106,000 Blood Money" are test canvases for the landscape of clashing armies in *Red Harvest.*
They are also excellent stories in themselves. As "The Big Knockover" opens, the Op passes information to a known con in a speakeasy. He enjoys the trust of criminals now, moving as easily among them as among the police. In fact, though he is tipped off to a huge bank robbery, the Op waits until the next day to inform his clients. As he approaches these banks the next morning, the Op sees a massive robbery in progress. Hammett introduces here a new and important motif—criminal gangs more powerful than the police, with leaders as rationally agile as the best detectives. After thirty-six dead bodies litter the initial pages, the possibility of society as leviathan emerges.

The female interest in the story is Angel Grace Cardigan, who appeared in the earlier "Second-Story Angel," a 1923 satire on pulp writers. Angel Grace is a crook with a code, a new kind of character; she believes in dealing fairly, but she "can't go over." Not nearly so honorable, the Op sets her up for a tail by Dick Foley. Meanwhile he and Counihan, a later version of Pat Reddy, trail Red O'Leary, the visible ringleader of the heist. He goes to a speakeasy, where they extricate him and his girl friend from a brawl. The way out is a peril of passages and halls; Hammett clearly liked the effect he had achieved in "Dead Yellow Women," for two men and a woman again achieve a crumbling moment of peace, a "promise of emptiness."

Outside the speakeasy, the Op finds it necessary to shoot O'Leary in the back surreptitiously to prevent him from fleeing. Then the Op accompanies him to a central hideout, the retreat of ringleaders Big Flora and Papadopoulos. The latter, a "shabby little old man" who follows Flora's orders, is the first in a series of sympathetic "rheumatic" or tubercular characters. Big Flora ties up the Op and puts him under the trembling gun of Papadopoulos. Convinced that the heist has been foiled, the old man arranges for the Op to capture O'Leary, then Pogey and Big Flora, in exchange for his freedom and Nancy Regan, O'Leary's girlfriend. Only after his departure does the Op learn that the innocuous old man is Papadopoulos, the mind behind the crime.

"The Big Knockover" is important because it is a long piece of writing, over 20,000 words, in which Hammett stretched Poe's boundary of the "tale" by linking a large number of crooks in one plot. To make the plot move, however, he had to kill off characters wholesale—at the end, there are fifty-eight known dead. This continued to be the problem with such plots, though Hammett was able to extend this one into a less bloody, equally effective sequel, "$106,000 Blood Money."

"$106,000 Blood Money" derives its narrative power from a series of betrayals, a theme of more interest than simple, benumbing murders. The story commences when Tom-Tom Carey announces to the Op that he intends to collect the $106,000 reward offered for Papadopoulos's capture. His ostensible motive is the murder of his brother, Paddy the Mex, in the bank robbery. But since he admits to betraying his brother, the theme of duplicity is established, and no character's motive is beyond suspicion. The Op strikes a deal with Tom-Tom: "If you turn in Papadopoulos I'll see that you get every nickel you're entitled to. . . . And I'll give you a clear field—I won't handicap you with too much of an attempt to keep my eyes on your actions" (*BK,* 417). This is the first time Hammett perceived that he could enlist reader sympathy in a deal between the Op and a crook; usually he opened with an account of the crime by one of the aggrieved.

The Op ties Tom-Tom almost immediately to the murder of millionaire Taylor Newhall, whose estate hires the Op to investigate. He pursues a number of false leads while Hammett introduces the cast required for the finale. Angel Grace Cardigan, Paddy the Mex's girl friend, tracks down Big Flora Brace, his killer, and befriends her. Jack Counihan, the dashing young operative of "The Big Knockover," leads the Op into a suspicious gunfight. Angel Grace and Big Flora break out of prison; Tom-Tom tracks them to Papadopoulos's hiding place, and alerts the Op that he is moving in.

Sending an operative to protect the nearby heiress of Taylor Newhall, the Op goes with Counihan and Tom-Tom to make the arrest. Linehan and Foley follow. When they approach the hideout they discover that Nancy Regan, Papadopoulos's co-escapee, is really Ann Newhall, the heiress. Sequestering her, they close in on the house. Counihan climbs a second story window to make the arrest, apparently without gunplay. When the Op, Tom-Tom, and the reserves arrive, Papadopoulos makes a break and Tom-Tom kills him.

The Op calls Counihan outside, and reveals to all—including the surprised reader—Jack's complicity with the crooks. His is the folly of having fallen in love with Nancy Regan/Ann Newhall. In a grilling as merciless as any he gives criminals, the Op reduces Counihan to ashes before the others. "The prospect of all that money completely devastated my morals," confesses Jack. But the Op will not settle for commonplaces. "You met the girl and were too soft to turn her in," he accuses. "But your vanity—your pride in looking at yourself as a pretty cold proposition—wouldn't let you admit it even to yourself. You had to have a hard-boiled front." With Counihan reduced, the Op "stood up straight and got rid of the last trace of my hypocritical sympathy" (*BK,* 455). He demands Counihan's gun, but the latter seems ready to shoot. Tom-Tom shoots first. Linehan, in turn, kills Tom-Tom. Then the Op reveals his unsuspected allegiance: "I stepped over Jack's body, went into the room, knelt down beside the swarthy man. He squirmed, tried to say something, died before he could get it out. I waited until my face was straight before I stood up." After a moment's reflection, it becomes clear that the Op regards Tom-Tom more highly than his fellow detective, that he has arranged the humiliation leading to Jack's death, and that he regards anyone who leaves himself open to sentiment or love as foolish. These are lessons that clarify Sam Spade's later decision about Brigid in *The Maltese Falcon.*

For the Op, however, the incident signals an end, because his superhuman ability to say what happens next has moved beyond self-mocking irony to an attack on his fellow questers that is only a step from self-destruction. In the story's last lines the Op says, "I felt tired, washed out." When he talks over the events with that superannuated office deity, the Old Man, the Op realizes that "for the first time in the years I had known him I knew what he was thinking. . . . 'It happened that way,' I said deliberately. 'I played the cards so that we could get the benefit of the breaks—but it just happened that way'" (*BK,* 455, 458). But of course the Op arranges it that way, and the fact that he does vitiates the allegoric level so much that, if he continues in this direction, Hammett will have to take up the problems of existentialism and absurdism. The Op will end here, because he has gotten too serious for popular culture.

Hammett's Style

The prose that Hammett discovered in the Op stories was at once deft and muscular, a style "that, at its best, was capable of saying anything," wrote Raymond Chandler. It has drawn praise from numerous critics because this prose practices, in few words, devices of tone, transition, and plot long thought to require more space. Many readers assume that Hammett's prose is simply the "tough talk" typical of American fiction in the 1920s. It is, but it goes beyond what previously existed. Tough

writing has been dissected with insight by Walker Gibson, who writes
that the tough narrator is in fact more concerned with "feelings than he is
with the outward scenes he presents, or with cultivating the good wishes of
the reader to whom he is introducing himself. He can ignore these
traditional services to the reader because he assumes in advance much
intimacy and common knowledge."[19]

Gibson sets up a number of tests, and Hammett—like Hemingway or
O'Farrell—meets all of them. His diction is characterized by short,
simple, largely Anglo-Saxon words. In a typical story his vocabulary is
77 percent monosyllabic, and only 2 percent of his words are not
Anglo-Saxon. Hammett's stress on clarity is manifest in Dick Foley, who
satirizes euphemisms such as "in conference," and "a victim of foul
play."

Hammett's prose aligns with other "tough talk" criteria: it features the
first-person pronoun, eschews the passive voice, and employs short
clauses. Hammett's average sentence, in his early work, is thirteen words
long. Highly descriptive passages run into flab at fifteen words. Fight
scenes are built of sentences averaging eight words each, some only three or
four words long.

> My arms had Maurois. We crashed down on dead Billie. I twisted around,
> kicking the Frenchman's face. Loosened one arm. Caught one of his. His other
> hand gouged at my face. That told me the bag was in the one I held. Clawing
> fingers tore at my mouth. I put my teeth in them and kept them there. One of
> my knees was on his face. I put my weight on it. My teeth still held his hand.
> Both of my hands were free to get the bag. (*CO,* 230)

These sentences were not only easy to read, but formed their own tiny
paragraphs in the narrow columns of the pulp format. The resulting white
spaces indicated a quickened pace of action. Later on Hammett wrote fight
scenes of remarkable rhythm, a sort of fistic poetry: "It was a swell bag of
nails. Swing right, swing left, kick, swing right, swing left, kick. Don't
hesitate, don't look for targets" (*BK,* 388).

The speed of this prose resides in its verbs. In a sample section of "The
Scorched Face," 20 percent of the words are verbs. They tend to be
simple and active, especially when the Op speaks or describes his actions,
and only compound or passive when Hammett characterizes the rich or
fills in a case history.

Hammett also gives the impression of eliding his story for his reader.
Time and space are compressed as the reader moves from scene to scene. If

the Op seeks information from someone windy or inarticulate, he summarizes the content: "I finally got it, but it cost me more words than I like to waste on incidentals." In "The Golden Horseshoe" the Op dashes to his "rooms for a bagful of clean clothes and went to sleep riding south again," thus spanning the distance between San Francisco and Mexico in a sentence (*CO,* 131, 69). No time is wasted on travel; essential detail after essential detail creates a sense of necessity in what comes next.

This speed allowed Hammett to write economical transitions. He often delays the revelation of a new scene until late in the transitional sentence, forcing the reader to absorb other information first. In "The Tenth Clew," for instance, "Half a dozen police detectives were waiting for us when we reached the detective bureau." When he is rescued from death in the Bay: "Half an hour later, shivering and shaking in my wet clothes, . . . I climbed into a taxi at the Ferry Building and went to my flat" (*CO,* 5, 35). Periodic sentences are a staple of good writing, but rarely has a writer used them so successfully to engage the reader in a new scene when he is expecting explication of the preceding one.

Equally deft are Hammett's creations of minor characters, an indispensable stock of detective fiction. At the beginning of "The Tenth Clew," he created and dismissed a butler in the same sentence, then passed two hours in twenty words. More celebrated, perhaps, are his descriptions of San Francisco. In reality these are spare and functional, setting important scenes, such as the Op's approach to Chinatown in "Dead Yellow Women":

Grant Avenue, the main street and spine of this strip, is for most of its length a street of gaudy shops and flashy chop-suey houses catering to the tourist trade, where the racket of American jazz orchestras drowns the occasional squeak of a Chinese flute. Farther out, there isn't so much paint and gilt, and you can catch the proper Chinese smell of spices and vinegar and dried things. If you leave the main thoroughfares and showplaces and start poking around in alleys and dark corners and nothing happens to you, the chances are you'll find some interesting things—though you won't like some of them. (*BK,* 207)

Hammett could achieve the effects appropriate to those "alleys and dark corners." The feeling of directionlessness in the Op's first trip to see Chang Li Ching's house is achieved by the sudden prevalence of the first-person pronoun without the usual emphatic verbs: "I was confused enough now, so far as the directions were concerned. I hadn't the least idea where I might be." When he required the reader to remember the topography of a locale for later action Hammett laid out the scene with scientific precision:

The White Shack is a large building, square-built of imitation stone. It is set away from the road, and is approached by two curving driveways, which, together, make a semi-circle whose diameter is the public road. The center of this semi-circle is occupied by sheds under which Joplin's patrons stow their cars, and here and there around the sheds are flower-beds and clumps of shrubbery. We were still going at a fair clip when we turned into one end of this semi-circular driveway. (*CO*, 155)

Such stylistic facility did not come automatically. An early draft of "The Sign of the Potent Pills" shows that the young Hammett was susceptible to editorializing and overwriting. He improved by rewriting and editing his old work.

The old man's

"Say no more," ~~old Newbrith cautioned her, even more significantly, and his~~ glance darted for a fleeting instant past ~~the younger man,~~ Trate.

and

Trate said something like, "Uh," shifted his feet uncertainly ~~and showed the Newbriths how utterly uncomprehending an otherwise attractive youthful face could be.~~

She gestured with champleve vial toward the door, and ~~Hugh, following the~~

stood

~~gesture with his eyes,~~ saw two men ~~standing~~ in that end of the room. One

opened the door

was the stolid man ~~who had admitted him to the house and to its subse-~~

He

~~quent peculiarities. Thisone, catching Hugh's eye,~~ nodded and grinned

at Trate

amiably.   [20]

It was a made, not a found, style. Some of its hallmarks seem dated—"I encouraged my brain with two Fatimas"—but it is a style that spoke to and for a large audience. "Hammett gave murder back to the kind of people that commit it for reasons, not just to provide a corpse; and with the means at hand, not hand-wrought dueling pistols, curare and tropical fish," wrote Raymond Chandler. "He put these people down on paper as they were, and he made them talk and think in the language they customarily used for these purposes. . . . Hammett's style at its worst was as formalized as a page of *Marius the Epicurean*; at its best it could say almost anything."[21]

Chapter Three

The *Black Mask* Novels

Red Harvest

At the end of February 1928, a manuscript arrived at the offices of publisher Alfred Knopf in New York. Since it came "over the transom" rather than from an agent, it joined similar manuscripts on a desk in a back corner. The publisher's wife, Blanche Knopf, who edited the firm's mystery series, sometimes read this "slush pile" for worthy material. Opening this particular package, she found a letter from Dashiell Hammett:

Herewith an action-detective novel for your consideration. If you don't care to publish it, will you kindly return it by express, collect.

By way of introducing myself: I was a Pinkerton's National Detective Agency operative for a number of years; and, more recently, have published fiction, book reviews, verse, sketches and so on, in twenty to twenty-five magazines, including the old Smart Set (when your Mssrs. Mencken and Nathan ran it), Forum, Bookman, Saturday Review, Life, Judge, Sunset, Argosy–Allstory, True Detective Mysteries, Black Mask (where "Poisonville" ran as a serial), Mystery Stories, Stratford, and Western Advertising.[1]

A few weeks later Mrs. Knopf wrote back that she had "read *Poisonville* with a great deal of interest." She suggested revisions: "There is no question, however, that we are keen about the mss., and with the necessary changes, I think that it would have a good chance."

Mrs. Knopf's critique suggested that the violence in "Poisonville," a title she disliked, might numb readers: "So many killings on a page I believe make the reader doubt the story, and instead of the continued suspense and feeling of horror, the interest slackens. . . ."[2]

Only eight days after Mrs. Knopf wrote her letter, Hammett returned all the revisions and a letter of his own. Against Mrs. Knopf's advice, he kept Lew Yard in the story, but he changed numerous scenes of violence, chapter titles, and the congested mid-section of the manuscript. He offered to make further revisions and submitted a list of eight titles, from which Mrs. Knopf chose *Red Harvest*. Hammett's letter concluded with a précis of his ambitions and plans, which reveals his continuing interest in "serious" fiction, now that he had found a reputable publisher:

> Then I want to try adapting the stream-of-consciousness method, conveniently modified, to a detective story, carrying the reader along with the detective, showing him everything as it is found, giving him the detective's conclusions as they are reached, letting the solution break on both of them together. I don't know whether I've made that very clear, but it's something altogether different from the method employed in Poisonville, for instance, where, though the reader goes along with the detective, he seldom sees deeper into the detective's mind than dialogue and action let him. . . .
>
> I'm one of the few—if there are any more—people moderately literate who take the detective story seriously. I don't mean that I necessarily take my own or anybody else's seriously—but the detective story as a form. Some day somebody's going to make "literature" of it (Ford's Good Soldier wouldn't have needed much altering to have been a detective story), and I'm selfish enough to have my hopes, however slight the evident justification may be. I have a long speech I usually make on the subject, all about the ground not having been scratched yet, and so on, but I won't bore you with it now.[3]

But by the beginning of April Hammett had already discovered Hollywood. His last letter of 1928 to Mrs. Knopf suggests that literary ambitions were not as immediately important as financial reward.

> I included RED HARVEST in the half a dozen stories submitted to the Fox Studio, and have hopes that something will come of it. In accordance with the terms of the contract, I shall, of course, pass on to you any offer Fox may make for RED HARVEST. If, as seems quite likely just now, I make more than a transient connection with Fox, I'll probably let the stream-of-consciousness experiment wait awhile, sticking to the more objective and filmable forms.
>
> Meanwhile, I'll have at you with another book next month.[4]

The editing of *Red Harvest* excised the stylistic and some of the thematic trademarks of *Black Mask,* which had published it as four stories: "The Cleansing of Poisonville" (November 1927); "Crime Wanted—Male or Female" (December 1927); "Dynamite" (January 1928); and "The 19th Murder" (February 1928). According to biographer Richard Layman, readers responded favorably to the series, which was set in the vicinity of Butte, Montana. Hammett knew the region well, having worked there as a Pinkerton during the labor troubles in the 1920s; and Jose Hammett had grown up in Anaconda, a company town outside Butte, and had visited again in 1924.

The Background of *Red Harvest*

The situation attracted Hammett's interest because it permitted a more complete rendering of the Hobbesian society that he had described in "The Big Knockover." Here were men fighting over primitive wealth, treasure in the ground—"enough of the combined metals to redeem the debts of all the nations of the earth," said one Anaconda president. The Western Federation of Miners had tried to organize the mines in 1912: at issue was a "rustling card" system that blackballed employees who incurred the displeasure of the bosses. When the W.F.M. failed, the more radical I.W.W. (Wobblies) stepped in. The Wobblies called a strike, made progress, but were stymied when the company marshaled patriotic sentiment behind it during World War I. Then Anaconda imported Pinkertons, strikebreakers, and gunmen to carry on a war against the Wobblies from 1917 until 1920. By then resistance had evaporated, leaving the town with a corps of avaricious mercenaries who seized the city government, the unions, the bootlegging, and gambling for themselves.

Such a state leads the characters in Hammett's novel to call their town "Poisonville," though its real name is Personville. The publisher of the town newspaper, Donald Willsson, sends for the Op, who is less jobholder than questing knight when removed from the company hierarchy. The Op's description of the town is probably the best opening in any of Hammett's novels:

The city wasn't pretty. Most of its builders had gone in for gaudiness. Maybe they had been successful at first. Since then the smelters whose brick stacks stuck up tall against a gloomy mountain to the south had yellow-smoked everything into uniform dinginess. The result was an ugly city of forty thousand people, set in an ugly notch between two ugly mountains that had been all dirtied up by mining. Spread over this was a grim sky that looked as if it had come out of the smelter's stacks.

The first policeman I saw needed a shave. The second had a couple of buttons off his shabby uniform. The third stood in the center of the city's main intersection—Broadway and Union Street—directing traffic, with a cigar in one corner of his mouth. After that I stopped checking them up.[5]

Donald Willsson is murdered before the Op can meet him. At first suspicion falls on his foreign-born wife, but an affable, decayed Wobblie named Bill Quint provides the Op with background on the city and its powerbrokers indicating that the murder figures in a power struggle around old Elihu Willsson, father of the victim and czar of the town. A personification of Anaconda, Elihu "won the strike, but he lost his hold on the city and the state. To beat the miners he had to let his hired thugs run wild." Quint reports that "The strongest of 'em now is probably Pete the Finn. This stuff we're drinking's his. Then there's Lew Yard. . . . Noonan, the chief of police. This kid Max Thaler—Whisper—has got a lot of friends too" (*RH*, 9–10).

The Op in *Red Harvest*

Elihu hires the Op to cleanse Poisonville after a gunman attempts to kill him too. The Op decides to set crook against crook. He establishes a working relationship with sultry, greedy Dinah Brand, who has scandalous information on most of the powerbrokers. Chief Noonan, who later attempts to kill the Op in a raid on Whisper's hideout, calls Dinah "a soiled dove, as the fellow says, a de luxe hustler, a big league gold-digger." She is one of Hammett's best minor characters, from whom the Op wins information only because he is tightfisted, can outdrink her, and resists her sexual advances. By the end of the first section, the Op puts a wedge between Whisper, whom he befriends, and Chief Noonan. The Willsson murderer, however, turns out to be Robert Albury, a bank employee jealous of the publisher's attentions to Dinah Brand.

The rationale for the second section is old Elihu's original broad agreement that the Op will "investigate crime and corruption in Personville." When one of Chief Noonan's policemen fires at the Op, and both Whisper and Old Elihu ask him to leave, the Op says: "I don't like that. I'm just mean enough to want to ruin [Noonan] for it. Now I'm going to have my fun. I've got ten thousand dollars of your money to play with. I'm going to use it opening up Poisonville from Adam's apple to ankles."

The Op's first action is to tamper with a prizefight that Whisper, a gambler, has rigged. The Op recognizes the "underdog" as a top boxer, who is wanted in the East for a bank robbery; he threatens to turn the boxer in if he takes a dive. The underdog wins, earning himself a knife in the back from one of Whisper's men. This divides Whisper, who loses money, and Dinah, who took the Op's tip. "So that's the way you scientific detectives work," she remarks. "Plans are all right sometimes," the Op says. "And sometimes just stirring things up is all right—if you're tough enough to survive, and keep your eyes open so you'll see what you want when it comes to the top" (*RH*, 60, 79).

When Dinah reports that "Max"—alias Whisper—killed Chief Noonan's brother years ago, the Op solicits a false confession from a witness. Whisper discovers that the Op is framing him, however, and jumps the Op and Dinah at her house. The second section ends with Whisper's capture by Chief Noonan.

Whisper's men dynamite the jail to free him and the Op finds the real killer is not "Max" but "MacSwain" at the beginning of the third section. Continental agents Foley and Linehan arrive to help out, but question the Op's failure to file reports. "It's right enough for the Agency to have rules and regulations," says the Op, "but when you're out on a job you've got to do it the best way you can. And anybody that brings any ethics to Poisonville is going to get them all rusty. A report is no place for the dirty details anyway, and I don't want you birds to send any writing back to San Francisco without letting me see it first" (*RH*, 109–10).

Linehan is assigned to Pete the Finn, Foley to Lew Yard. Back in Chief Noonan's good graces, the Op goes on a raid of the Cedar Hill Inn, where Whisper is supposedly hiding. They destroy a cache of Pete the Finn's liquor, but meanwhile Whisper robs Old Elihu's First National Bank. Then the Op befriends a con named Reno Starkey, who is modelled on Tom-Tom in "$106,000 Blood Money." He sets him against Lew Yard, who is killed. The third section ends when Noonan, sickened by the killing, asks the Op to arrange a peace conference.

Action in the final section stems from the Op's mounting tension. "This burg's getting me," he says. "If I don't get away soon I'll be going blood simple like the natives." He succumbs to Dinah's offer to dose his drink with laudanum and begins to ramble: "I've arranged a killing or two in my time, when they were necessary. But this is the first time I've ever got the fever. It's this damned burg. You can't go straight here. I got myself tangled at the beginning. . . . I had to swing the job the best way I could. How could I help it if the best way was bound to lead to a lot of killing?" (*RH*, 142–43). In the drugged sleep that follows, the Op has two important dreams; but when he wakes, Dinah is dead, an icepick in her back. The Op gets an alibi from Reno Starkey, then feverishly plays off the criminals against each other.

Whisper kills Noonan, and is in turn wounded by Dan Rolff, a consumptive "lunger" modeled on Hammett himself, who lives on Dinah's charity. An excellent minor character, Rolff is twisted by his addiction to laudanum, and his jealousy motivates the novel's finale. A warrant appears for the Op's arrest, which forces him to dismiss the suspicious Dick Foley. The Op and Reno bomb Pete the Finn's warehouse, shooting the gangleader as he surrenders. Meanwhile Whisper's men, believing their leader is inside, attack the jail, which Pete's men defend.

When the Op hands Personville back to Old Elihu, he says: "You're going to have the mayor, or the governor, whichever it comes under, suspend the whole Personville police department and let the mail-order troops handle things until you can organize another. I'm told that the mayor and the governor are both pieces of your property. They'll do what you tell them. And that's what you're going to tell them."

The Op gives weight to his order by threatening to publish Elihu's love letters to Dinah. Then he and Linehan seek the hideout of Whisper; they find Dan Rolff and Whisper dead and Reno dying. Though he admits that he killed Dinah, Reno elicits the Op's admiration: "He meant to die as he had lived, inside the same tough shell. Talking could be torture, but he wouldn't stop on that account. He was Reno Starkey who could take anything the world had without batting an eye, and he would play it that way to the end" (*RH,* 187, 197).

Allegory in *Red Harvest*

All the devices of plot and characterization that Hammett used in *Red Harvest* had been pretested in the Op stories. Considerably different, however, is the environment, its scale, and its effect on the Op. From the first page, there is a sense that the remote Montana town is at once a world apart and an amoral microcosm of America. It is singularly bleak. Even the Old Man, the etiolated deity of the Op's office-worker world, never establishes his reign here. Order was the underlying premise of the Op stories, but chaos is the topography of Personville. The reader meets no Pat Reddy or Effie Perrine; everyone in allegorically named Personville is emblematic of some sin.

To chaos the Op must bring order. His cynicism and suspicion are more concentrated and bitter than they were in San Francisco, as his brutal interrogations of Albury and Mrs. Willsson attest. Unimpeachably hard, the Op dismisses or leaves to fate the few sympathetic characters; he must adopt local "means." This characterization comes from an earlier story, "The Hunter," in which Hammett revealed the Op's thoughts only to admit his callousness. In *Red Harvest* the Op tells the reader that he is lying twice in the first five pages. Subsequently he notes in passing that "I lied out of it," "I gave him a name," "I looked most honest when lying," "I lied," and "I . . . tried to look virtuous as hell" (*RH,* 5, 7, 102, 156, 136). The first person narration works only outward: to build a character who seems to be of the tough, vicious world of professional crime. The Op reduces all personality and events to the common denominators of the criminal world, through which he moves with practiced ease.

But the reader is drawn to the Op, because only a man familiar with the depths of evil is capable of eradicating it. That the Op is a moral quester is clear, because he pays a price, gets the "fever," typical ways of signaling the knight-hero's difference from his peers. He may lie, and may arrange for criminals to kill one another, but the Op recognizes the good in Robert Albury, Dan Rolff, and Ted Wright. He may not feel remorse for the deaths of the boxer or "burly Nick," but he finds their killers. A sense of accumulated past sin weights and justifies the deaths of those he kills. Hammett keeps the Op seemingly moral in this avaricious world by making him unswervingly devoted to one point of his code: he cannot be bought. He does not squander the Agency's resources. He does "honest work" for his pay, and his repeated refusals to give Dinah money epitomize this ethos. His adherence to this single point permits his adaptability on all others. In a Hobbesian world a single principle makes a hero.

Hammett discovered in the Op stories that the more allegoric functions the hero had, the more necessary it was they be masked by human foibles. In *Red Harvest* he invented a shorthand for the foibles: he humanized the Op by his confession that he had "succumbed" to Poisonville. "Play with murder enough," he remarks, "and it gets you one of two ways. It makes you sick or you get to like it":

Look. I sat at Willsson's table tonight and played them like you'd play trout, and got just as much fun out of it. I looked at Noonan and knew he hadn't a chance in a thousand of living another day because of what I had done to him, and I laughed, and felt warm and happy inside. That's not me. I've got hard skin all over what's left of my soul, and after twenty years of messing around with crime I can look at any sort of a murder without seeing anything in it but my bread and butter, the day's work. But this getting a rear out of planning deaths is not natural to me. It's what this place has done to me. (*RH,* 145)

The humanizing element here is environmental determinism: the hero understandably loses his morality in a murderous milieu. Layman calls this confession the Op's "crucial mistake"; another scholar thinks "we feel with the Op the horror of his joy in setting up deaths." The first recognizes the allegoric, the second the appeal to the reader. Clearly Hammett needs a sense of narrative urgency to bind together the quester and the realist at this point. Confession is an act the two could share, and the laudanum makes plausible the dreams that unify the levels of the story.

In the first dream the Op meets a veiled woman, "somebody I knew well," who vanishes. He walks the streets of the United States looking for her; he hears her voice, but can never get any nearer. When he finally stops, she appears and begins to kiss him. "I was very uncomfortable because everyone stood around looking at us and laughing," he notes.

In the second dream the Op is a man-hunter, chasing a "small brown man who wore an immense sombrero." He has an open knife in his pocket, and the chase leads away from a cathedral over the "heads and shoulders of the people in the plaza." He chases the man to the top of a building, seizes him by the head, and realizes "that I had gone off the edge of the roof with him" (*RH,* 150, 151).

Though psychoanalytic interpretation might yield interesting results, the dreams have two pedestrian functions meant to be readily available to readers. They describe a "coked up" version of Dinah's murder, the details of which Reno Starkey later makes clear. Dinah had been talking to Whisper on the phone and to Reno at the door, going in and out; this is the distorted reality in the first dream. When Reno stabs Dinah, the Op jumps up from his revery and charges, but he falls down on Dinah, grasping the bulbous handle of the ice pick. This action, rearranged, provides the imagery of the second dream. Unaware of the real actions when the dreams are recounted, the reader apprehends only similarities and contrasts. Both dreams are quests, the first after a personal emotional life that ends in embarrassment; the second after a man (reflecting the Op's occupation) that ends in death. Both have an immediately apparent sentimental value, which is one function. But, taken sequentially, the allegoric function is to imply that the admission of emotion leads to death. The hero has been warned, as heroes of the grail often are, by "supernatural" means after taking a "potion." Since this dream is the reader's single sustained view of the Op's consciousness, it appropriately unites his two functions. Its success is noteworthy. In later books Hammett attempted to create similarly compelling bridges between the quest and the realistic, and usually he failed.

As an allegory *Red Harvest* is unfinished: order does not rise from chaos; it is simply a possibility now. The evildoers have been dispatched, but little has been affirmed. The reader notices only that the Op never again "succumbs," or needs emotional rest. The pressures on him build when the warrant for his arrest appears, but he does not falter. By returning the love letters to Elihu, he seems in fact to extend to him an emotional relief not personally available. To close the moral scheme Hammett draws on his Catholic background. By the process of atonement, the Op makes himself fit for the world. "I spent most of my week in Ogden trying to fix up my reports so they would not read as if I had broken as many Agency rules, state laws and human bones as I had." Out there, in the orderly work-a-day world, the organizational deity still prevails: "They didn't fool the Old Man. He gave me merry hell" (*RH*, 199).

Responses to *Red Harvest*

There are technical flaws in *Red Harvest*, though few of them have bothered readers as the level of violence has. Conspicuous in several spots is the lack of "necessity" requisite to detective fiction. Hammett had a difficult time, in revision, of reweaving the plot to connect the four original stories. This is most obvious after the first section, for the death of Donald Willsson lacks connection to the warfare in Personville. The murderer apprehended, the Op should leave; it requires a sudden eruption of vengeance on his part to create a bridge to the second section. The fight fixing is also a marvellous short story that does little for the plot. Hammett sensed the lack of necessity, and early on provided the Op with the rationale of "stirring things up." But aside from the bogus "peace conference" that he arranges, the Op only stirs a little. More often he accompanies Chief Noonan or Reno on raids, describing the violence that ensues.

It is the compelling sense of present action, of "things breaking fast," that makes the carnage so vivid to readers, but violence reaches potentially objectionable levels only in chapter 24, "Whiskeytown," in which Reno bombs Pete the Finn's warehouse and then murders him as he surrenders. The Knopf editors tried to help with this and other problems. Harry Block, apparently the "reader" who recommended deleting some of the bombings, dynamitings, and killings, did the close editing of the manuscript. A thorough and meticulous editor, he left few sentences untouched. He substituted nouns for pronouns and expanded many contractions. He cut phrases and reordered sentences. Of the content, he seems to have changed only dates, which he made less specific than in the serial, and a few of the names of characters and places.[6]

Red Harvest was not an immediate success, though its reviews at the time of publication were acceptable and improved later. Knopf's initial press run of about 3,000 copies lasted through 1929. A second printing did not appear until March 1930, and there was a third printing in 1931, when *The Glass Key* came out. *Red Harvest* appeared in Knopf's new Borzoi line of mysteries, considered the most literary of such series. The book sold for $2.50, more money than most people could devote to 60,000 words of entertainment during the depression.[7]

Reviewers liked the dialogue and characterization especially. Walter Brooks wrote in the *Outlook and Independent* that "a thriller that lives up to the blurb on the jacket is unusual enough to command respect. When, in addition, it is written by a man who plainly knows his underworld and can make it come alive for his readers, when the action is exciting and the conversation racy and amusing—well, you'll want to read it. . . ." In the *Bookman* Herbert Asbury wrote, "It is doubtful if even Ernest Hemingway has ever written more effective dialogue than may be found within the pages of this extraordinary story of gunmen, gin and gangsters . . . the liveliest detective story that has been published in a decade."

It was many years later that *Red Harvest* attracted attention for changes it wrought in the genre. A *Saturday Review* writer said that detection had "moved out from the back room of the pulps into the bright light of the best bookstores" with the hardcover printing of *Red Harvest*. "The private eye was stepping forward to claim his kingdom," wrote the reviewer. Critic Martin Maloney noted that the old image of the detective had been destroyed: "It is a long step from Holmes pondering the significance of a flake of cigar ash . . . to Hammett's Op, who, on one occasion stuffs a length of copper wire into his pocket because it's just the right length to go around somebody's neck. The verb 'to pursue' now becomes . . . 'to destroy' . . . and the black-and-white universe of Holmes vanishes. . . . The burden of guilt for crime tends to spread, so that no one is free of it."[8]

The poet Robert Graves later called *Red Harvest* "an acknowledged literary landmark." Andre Gide said it was "the last word in atrocity, cynicism and horror . . . a remarkable achievement," the dialogue of which ranked "with the best in Hemingway." What fueled some of this latter round of admiration, however, was the notion that *Red Harvest* was really a Marxist critique of capitalism, corrupt unionism, and the abuse of power by elected officials. That Hammett had any of these notions in mind when he wrote it is doubtful: as Richard Layman notes, there is no evidence of class conflict, and "there are no masses of politically dispossessed people." But Hammett did know his way around Butte and Anaconda.[9]

The Dain Curse

The Dain Curse is a novel of sophisticated intent, written when Hammett was at peak power, that nevertheless disappoints readers. Its picture of the world of California religious cults—the first such in American literature—is familiar by now. And the unusual twists that it gives to the grail myth and the conventions of the detective novel are usually lost by readers struggling with the long, complex plot.

The plot suffers, again, from its origin as four separate stories in *Black Mask*, whose editors did not believe in continuations. Yet the four plots are united by Hammett's search for a way to hold his hero and "loathly lady" in the dramatic tension that he had discovered in "The Girl with the Silver Eyes." He was not to find that vehicle until *The Maltese Falcon*. Gabrielle Dain Leggett, the beautiful woman of *The Dain Curse*, stands in this relation to the Op, but she is equally a traditional damsel in distress.

The Op is called to the Leggett home to investigate a theft of diamonds from scientist Edgar Legget. After interviewing Mrs. Leggett and the disagreeable Gabrielle, he learns that a former friend, the writer and eventual villain Owen Fitzstephan, has returned to San Francisco. Patient legwork and aid from his agency's East Coast bureau allow the Op to pin the robbery on Upton and Ruppert, two former detectives gone bad. Distressed by the turmoil, Gabrielle, a morphine addict, flees to the Temple of the Holy Grail. Her fiancé Eric Collinson and the Op retrieve her, but return home to find Fitzstephan and Mrs. Leggett standing over Leggett's body. In a suicide note Leggett identifies himself as an escaped French criminal, guilty of murdering his first wife and now prey to an extortion by Upton and Ruppert. The Op parses the crimes differently; he accuses Mrs. Leggett of the murder. In her vindictive reply she reveals that she coached Gabrielle to kill her mother, then forced Edgar to take the blame and to marry her. Gabrielle's addiction, she adds, is the result of this and a Dain family curse. In the following confusion, she is killed in a scuffle with Fitzstephan and the Op.

The second and most interesting section of the novel takes place in Joseph and Aaronia Haldorn's Temple of the Holy Grail, a cult that the Op identifies as a "revival of an old Gaelic Church, dating to King Arthur's time." When Gabrielle flees there a second time, her guardian dispatches the Op to watch over her. To the Op's surprise he falls asleep his first night on the job, and on waking finds his client gone. When he locates her, Gabrielle has a bloody dagger in hand—her physician, Dr. Riese, is dead. The suspicious Op goes to another room seeking a more likely culprit, but is overcome by hallucinogenic fumes, and does battle with an illusion. He vanquishes it, but Gabrielle escapes. The Op finds her with Joseph, the cult leader, who is about to kill Aaronia on the cult's stone altar because he prefers Gabrielle. The Op stops the maniacal leader with seven bullets and a dagger in the neck. "I saw them go in," he says, "I drove the heavy blade into his throat, in till the hilt's cross stopped it."[10]

Part three moves to Quesada, a town eighty miles south of San Francisco modeled on Monterey. Eric Collinson has taken Gabrielle there for a honeymoon after a quick marriage in Nevada; they stay in a cottage recommended by Fitzstephan, whose link to the murders begins to look suspicious. Collinson sends for the Op, who arrives to find him dead and Gabrielle gone. He reports the death and disappearance, but finds the town's legal apparatus as diseased as that of the big city: the sheriff, the district attorney, and the marshall battle each other for power and publicity. The death of the marshall's adulterous wife finally provides a clue that leads a posse to a hidden coastal cove, where one Harvey Whidden holds Gabrielle for ransom. He is killed resisting arrest, a solution that does not satisfy the Op, who returns to Fitzstephan's apartment to talk about it. There a bomb explodes, mangling the writer but not harming the Op.

In the fourth section, which is a shortened revision of the *Black Mask* story, the Op attempts to cure Gabrielle of morphine addiction. Sequestering her at the Quesada cottage, he feigns an attraction and sees her through delirium tremens. As she recovers, the Op warns off both Madison Andrews, the guardian who is dipping into her inheritance, and Aaronia Haldorn, who is seducing Andrews to gain control of the estate. Then the Op confronts the crippled Fitzstephan with evidence that he arranged or committed all the murders. Fitzstephan gives a tacit confession—he too is a Dain, like Gabrielle—but vows that he will claim insanity in court. He does and is later exonerated, but the Op feels vindicated because Gabrielle is a vibrant young woman, while Fitzstephan can no longer distinguish between reality and illusion.

Aside from general agreement that the plot, given in much simplified form here, is overwrought and suffers gaps where the original stories ended, no consensus exists about the source of the novel's disappointment. One critic argues that "the characters are entirely at the service of the plot," and another that "the characterization of the Op is the strength of the novel." A third thinks the novel a microcosm of *Red Harvest,* a *famille noir* in which lust rather than greed is the most damning sin.[11]

Technique in *The Dain Curse*

The fact that *The Dain Curse* sustains these differing views seems indicative of a richer content than its customary dismissal would indicate. Even skeptics admit that *The Dain Curse* contains passages of Hammett's best writing, but few critics have remarked on Hammett's ambitious experiment with detective conventions and typology in this novel. *The Dain Curse* is the book of an impatient writer, who chafes at his generic restrictions; its consideration should begin with the remark Hammett made in his letter to Mrs. Knopf: "I want to try adapting the stream-of-consciousness method, conveniently modified, to a detective story, carrying the reader along with the detective . . . letting the solution break on both of them together."[12]

Stream of consciousness is a narrative technique in which the thoughts and actions of the point-of-view character are presented as one continuous flow, rather than as discrete actions. To use it in a detective novel, where evidence presented to the reader must be reliable, would mean sacrificing the subjectivity that is one of its advantages. Only in a few sections did Hammett find he could employ the technique per se, but he found other new ways to open the detective's ratiocinative process to the reader. "I piled up what facts I had, put some guesses on them, and took a jump from the top of the heap into space," the Op says. Frequently the descriptions signal that he is moving from fact to speculation. When he accuses Alice Leggett of her husband's murder, for example, he notes: "Her face didn't tell me anything. It was distorted, but in a way that might have meant almost anything. I filled my lungs and went on, not exactly bellowing, but getting plenty of noise out." Later he describes this technique again: "I didn't give her a chance to answer any of these questions but sailed ahead, turning my voice loose" (*DC,* 51–52). Hammett gives signs when the Op is moving from given facts to solutions that the reader can infer. His solutions draw on no undisclosed evidence or special knowledge, as do resolutions in most traditional mysteries. The rule of the genre that all evidence be presented to the reader has rarely been observed as scrupulously as in *The Dain Curse.*

Actual stream of consciousness is employed principally in the Temple scenes. In previous work Hammett had used short sentences with grammatical necessity (hypotaxis) to describe situations of peril or action. He uses this tactic in the novel, but when he seeks to show the influence of chloroform on the Op he employs parataxis—long sentences in which related clauses have an elliptic, disconnected quality:

Looking at her, I felt drowsy myself. It seems a shame to turn her out. Perhaps she was dreaming of—I shook my head, trying to clear it of the muddle settling there. Lilies of the valley, moonflowers—flowers that had died—was honeysuckle one of the flowers? The question seemed to be important. The flashlight was heavy in my hand, too heavy. Hell with it: I let it drop. It hit my foot, puzzling me: who had touched my foot? Gabrielle Leggett, asking to be saved from Eric Collinson? That didn't make sense, or did it? I tried to shake my head again, tried desperately. It weighed a ton, and would barely move from side to side. (DC, 81)

Although the passage in which the Op fights the ghost has been scored for implausibility, it is well written, describing in the most objective terms an impalpable vision:

Not more than three feet away, there in the black room, a pale bright thing like a body, but not like flesh, stood writhing before me. It was tall, yet not so tall as it seemed, because it didn't stand on the floor, but hovered with its feet a foot or more above the floor. Its feet—it had feet, but I don't know what their shape was. They had no shape, just as the thing's legs and torso, arms and hands, head and face, had no shape, no fixed form. They writhed, swelling and contracting, stretching and shrinking, not greatly, but without pause.

As the Op remarks a few pages later, "The ghost had me sweating ink" (DC, 82, 97).

Hammett also experimented with his point of view in *The Dain Curse.* His first-person detective-narrator was already an exception: tradition from Poe through Doyle and Sayers dictated that the detective's adventures be explained by a first-person acquaintance neither as smart nor as eccentric as the detective. The Watson allows readers to feel bright and adventurous, since they see answers that he does not, but his bafflement is reassuring when they do not see the solution. Hammett had already thrown over the tradition with a first-person detective-narrator who told the reader what he was seeing, hearing, and thinking. His eccentricity or brilliance became less important than his fidelity to a chivalric code in a lawless world.

But Hammett also, in clever fashion, reinstitutes the Watson convention. One function of this character is to engage the sleuth in speculation about the crime and its solution. This job Hammett assigned to Owen Fitzstephan, the villain. He assumes the eccentric characteristics that traditionally belong to the detective: he knows about abnormal psychology and the occult, he is a sensualist and an epicure. He volunteers to borrow a book or to delay a suspect so the detective may be elsewhere. In the speculative conversations, Fitzstephan argues for the fantastic explanation. He is disappointed that the Op can reduce the "Dain curse" to "a primitive strain in the blood."

Yet Hammett deliberately made the writer an attractive character, with whom readers are invited to identify for most of the novel. There is a nice twist in this; by providing a Watson, who assumes Holmes's characteristics, and by then incriminating him, Hammett indicts readers who identify with Holmes's esoteric reasoning. In effect, readers choose and are responsible for their choices when the attendant characteristics are revealed to drive the criminal. The impulse behind the technique is almost homiletic, pointing to the importance of personal responsibility.

This inventiveness finds other playful outlets. All of the early conversations between the Op and Fitzstephan radiate an awareness that the fictional detective and the fictional novelist engage in the same activity. The description of Fitzstephan matches that of Hammett: "a long, lean sorrel-haired man of thirty-two, with sleepy gray eyes, a wide, humorous mouth, and carelessly worn clothes; a man who pretended to be lazier than he was, would rather talk than do anything else, and had a lot of what seemed to be accurate information and original ideas on any subject that happened to come up." His apartment, like Hammett's, is littered with newspapers, books, and proof sheets. In the meeting that reacquaints them, Fitzstephan accuses the Op of speaking in "proprietary" tones, like "one who has bought an author for a couple of dollars." He asks if the detective is "still hounding the unfortunate evildoer," an allusion to Chang Li Ching in "Dead Yellow Women" (*DC,* 22–23).

Hammett alerts his readers to this duplicity when the Op tells Fitzstephan, "You're a story-writer. I can't trust you not to build up on what I tell you. I'll save mine until after you've spoken your piece, so yours won't be twisted to fit mine." The reader must remember that, as the Op says, he and Fitzstephan "drink out of the same bottle" (*DC,* 23, 19). Both are engaged in the creation of a "reality." Although Fitzstephan insists that his "primary business is with souls and what goes on in them," his activity is no different than that of the Op, who says, "I spent most of the afternoon putting my findings and guesses on paper and trying to fit them together in some sort of order." What Hammett does for the first time in *The Dain Curse* is to incorporate on the periphery of the narrative the fact that part of the detective's work is to make fictions. As Steven Marcus writes, it is "a discovery or creation by fabrication of something new in the world, or hidden, latent, potential, or as yet undeveloped within it."[13]

This playfulness appears in a number of ways. Just before the bomb explodes, Fitzstephan touts the resolutions of Nick Carter mysteries over the methods of the Op. Eric Collinson's very name is a joke, one of Hammett's old pennames and a common underworld alias. Other in-jokes turn on the diamond business and Albert Samuels, to whom the novel is dedicated: Samuels told an interviewer that Leggett was his switchboard operator, Riese was another employee, and Mrs. Priestly was in silverware. Another series of puns, in which Collinson is called "the Chevalier Bayard," refers to Bayard Sartoris in William Faulkner's *Sartoris,* published as Hammett was rewriting.

Chaffing Against the Genre

Most of Hammett's invention was applied to the genre. If the traditional detective story was set in the English countryside, and the Hammett inversion of it in the urban sink, then in *The Dain Curse* the crimes would occur in suburbia, in cults, and in small towns. In the traditional story, the cast was limited and one of its number the murderer; Hammett swelled his actors to twenty-eight, moving them on and off stage freely. None have apparent motives, another traditional staple, and the only solid evidence—the two suicide notes—is "fiction," erroneous versions of reality that the Op must interpret.

As this indicates, Hammett was very self-conscious about writing within a genre. That the genre was not accorded the "serious" regard that his contemporaries Hemingway and Faulkner received and that it drew its power from claims about reality that a man of Hammett's materialist views should not endorse further bothered him. "When Hammett described himself as a writer," notes his biographer, "the unspoken qualification that he was a *pulp mystery writer* always irritated him. He strained to maintain his dignity as an author, to let it be known that he wasn't just another pulp hack."[14] By 1929 he began to feel permanently typed, his only escape the hope of raising his performance to the level of his famous contemporaries'.

One way *The Dain Curse* differs from Hammett's preceding work is that it gives attention to the problem of "knowing what is real," which is simply assumed by most detective novels. The complex plot tends to obscure this consideration, as do the bizarre characters. But reflect a moment: only the Op *knows* what reality is in *The Dain Curse*. Fitzstephan is insane, Leggett is paranoid, Mrs. Leggett is a sociopath, and Gabrielle is stupefied by drugs. By locating the crimes in a mystic world and by blaming an insane villain, Hammett made his Op not only the semidivine agent of justice but the arbiter of reality. That the Op destroys some fictions to raise a greater fiction of his own—real "reality"—is an irony Hammett may or may not have intended.

This theme is set out in the first words of the novel. "It was a diamond all right." The reader, like the Op, is to be suspicious of appearance, to debate with the Op the genuineness of Leggett's Oriental rug, to notice that Leggett's work—he seeks to give imperfect diamonds an artificially heightened color—is a conflict of appearance and reality. The "stolen" diamonds are in fact a concocted "robbery."

All flight from the Op's "real reality" is punished. When the Op and Collinson rescue Gabrielle, Collinson's obstinacy causes a crash. When Mrs. Leggett assents to Fitzstephan's fiction about the "suicide note," she dies. Fitzstephan himself is blown up. Even a minor character like Madison Andrews, the libido-ridden lawyer, is corrected in emasculating terms that he understands. Each is punished according to his illusion.

This theme has two culminations: first, the Op battles chloroform visions in the temple; second, he cures Gabrielle of addiction. The thematic importance of the Op's exploits in the temple becomes clear when he discovers that he has fallen asleep. A puff of "real" air rouses him, and the Op "has sense enough" to reach for the light switch: "Light scorched my eyes. Squinting, I could see a world that was real to me, and could remember that I had work to do. I made for the bathroom, where cold water on head and face left me still stupid and muddled, but at least partly conscious." The basically physical nature of reality is evident. The Op's certitude is based on past experience with deception, and his awareness of a certain psychic fulcrum, at which, under extreme stress, people drop their illusions. He sheds tears when he himself comes to that point: "Air that stung like ammonia came through the opening. I put my face to it, hanging to the sill with both hands, sucking air in through mouth, nose, eyes, ears and pores, laughing with water from my stinging eyes trickling into my mouth. I hung there drinking air until I . . . knew myself able to think and move again" (*DC,* 73, 82).

Like the heroes of the grail tales, the Op must vanquish a personal demon, "that which had no shape, no fixed form." This demon is an avatar of the Temple's mysticism, made more potent because, as the Op notes, he "didn't believe in the supernatural—but what of that? The thing was there and it was not, I knew, a trick of luminous paint, a man with a sheet over him."

When his senses betray him, the Op retreats to his psychic fulcrum: "I was there and the thing was there, and I stayed where I was." Unintimidated by visions, certain that all is matter, the Op sights victory when the illusion orders him to submit. "An argument was something I understood," he says: "I moved my handkerchief sufficiently to say: 'Go to hell'" (*DC,* 83). The Op "understands" the command because it is a hypothesis about the physical world.

That Hammett should limit ultimate reality to a physical world is not surprising; both his reading and his knockabout life inclined him to a strict materialism. Moreover he had the self-educated American's distrust of values not directly related to *facts.* This puts him in the awkward position of claiming that only his hero, of all the characters in *The Dain Curse,* really knows the nature of reality. Yet this is a claim that detection, almost alone among genres, will tolerate. Hammett substantiates it by the Op's past exploits and his battle with the illusion.

By this time Hammett saw that a hero who is both arbiter of the real and author of the clues, has assumed for himself God-like power. He set up the interplay between the Op and Fitzstephan to point out his ironic awareness of the power that he manipulated. When Fitzstephan says to the Op, "Do you admit you've met your master, have run into a criminal too wily for you?" Hammett is winking at the reader, as he did in "Dead Yellow Women."

The Op's attempt to cure Gabrielle of her addiction is the summation of the "reality" theme, an exorcism of the mysticism that has afflicted her. When Gabrielle argues that her "curse" prevents her from "thinking" clearly, the Op discourses on the nature of thought: "Nobody thinks clearly, no matter what they pretend. Thinking's a dizzy business, a matter of catching as many of those foggy glimpses as you can and fitting them together the best you can." This imperfect process is nonetheless critical, says the Op. It is not speculation, but an apprehension of how the "glimpses" join on a primal level: "And if you let it get away from you, then you've got to dive back into that foggy muddle to wangle yourself out another to take its place" (*DC,* 138, 149).

It seems clear that for the Op, the "foggy glimpses" of fact become obscured if held long on the plane of abstraction. That they fit together in immediately apprehensible ways, and not far above the realm in which they are discovered, owes to the connecting tissue—most often something as basic as lust, greed, addiction, or hatred. Thinking also requires discipline. Diving "back into that foggy muddle" is self-correction, a forced refresher in these common denominators. The Op warns also against introspection: "Evidence of goofiness is easily found: the more you dig into yourself, the more you turn up."

The seriousness and consistency of this probe break down when the Op, whose argument rested on an assumption of free will, argues the determinist side of the question. And a third perspective appears when Gabrielle asks, "Aren't there people who are so thoroughly . . . evil that they poison . . . everybody they touch?" (*DC*, 150–51). The likelihood is that Hammett believed all his arguments to some degree; it is hard to fault him for failing to answer, in an entertainment, a question of such magnitude.

Portraying California Cults

Hammett was the first popular American novelist to pay attention to cults and their leaders. His source was undoubtedly his environment: California attracted the spiritually footloose, and the 1920s witnessed the introduction of Eastern literatures and religious texts into the United States on a mass scale. The unprecedented prosperity of the decade seemed to herald a spiritual expansion as well, with California in the forefront. Raymond Chandler later recognized the fecundity of the theme in *Farewell My Lovely*, in which Phillip Marlowe is stymied by "psychic consultant" Jules Amthor. And Ross McDonald, in *The Moving Target*, notes that Lew Archer fears "slipping off the edge of a case into a fairy tale" when he visits a cult called the Temple of the Clouds.

Hammett laid out for all who followed a method of involving readers in the cult's terrors. He begins with a description of the pastel California landscape, inducing ease and calm, rather than detailing the urban pressures that breed cults. The setting seems spiritually dull, in fact, except for the "progressive" activities of the cult. Its devotees are usually young, attractive, female, and at odds with their elders.

A credible bystander like Collinson, who does not belong, introduces the point-of-view character and the reader to the cult's workings. "It isn't hocus-pocus really," he says. "I don't know very much about their creed, or anything like that, but I've been to their services, with Gabrielle, and they're quite as dignified, as beautiful even, as either Episcopalian or Catholic services."

The surroundings are disarmingly normal, even attractive: "the rug was soft and thick, and what I could see of the furniture leaned towards luxury rather than severity. . . . 'I wouldn't mind moving in here myself,' I told Collinson" (*DC*, 38–40).

Other endorsements follow. Dr. Riese declares the cult harmless; Madison Andrews, the lawyer, notes the upper-class membership and says, "We are not concerned with its religious aspects. We're interested in it as therapeutics, as a cure for Gabrielle's mind" (*DC*, 65). A web of approval is woven around a group the reader previously thought taboo.

Until this plausibility can be established, the cult holds no danger for the reader, so it is important that the novelist withhold the appearance of the leader. No guru can charm all readers and a basically skeptical hero. A great difference in appearance and manners may be permitted him, but when he violates the American law that one man's as good as another, the events of the narrative begin to move against him. Hammett made this reversal look easy:

Joseph Haldorn was tall, built like a statue, and wore a black silk robe. His hair was thick, long, white and glossy. His thick beard, trimmed round, was white and glossy. Aaronia Haldorn introduced me to him, calling him "Joseph" as if he had no last name. All of the others addressed him in the same way. He gave me a white even-toothed smile and a warm strong hand. His face, healthily pink, was without line or wrinkle. It was a tranquil face, especially the clear brown eyes, somehow making you feel at peace with the world. The same soothing quality was in his baritone voice.

"It wasn't so bad," says the Op. "I said that I, too, was happy to be there, and while I was saying it I actually thought I was" (*DC*, 70).

The entry into the cult leads the reader to a discovery about evil that approximates an intuition confirmed: appearances are deceptive. Only the Op, ever suspicious, is prepared when the Haldorns attempt to chloroform him into discipledom. He recurs to history, comparing the hallway as he saw it earlier with the hallway as he sees it. He puts himself *in time,* looking at his watch and calculating the hours elapsed. The deceptiveness of first impressions is the heart of all anticult wisdom; only by living in time, history, obligations, and codes can one know "reality" and be happy.

The explanation of the illusion in the denouement of the second section seems long to readers rafting along the plot line. But it deflates cults further. The Op explains that the Haldorns were originally actors—not good actors, but failures who wanted to "ride in Packards instead of day-coaches." They got their cult from Arthur Machen, an actual English occultist *(The Great God Pan)*. To provide the illusions, they hired a man who had "been in charge of the mechanical end of most of the well-known stage magicians and illusionist's acts." The mystic becomes less than mechanical; and the reader is embarrassed that he laid aside his suspicion. You may be sure he will not do so again.

The Dain Curse points finally to the emptiness of the modern American spiritual condition, showing the distance to which the faithless will go to find significance. This movement involves the reader, as well, in a quest for fulfillment that is typical of romances following the grail pattern. "The detective-knight," notes George Grella, "must journey to a Perilous Chapel where an ambivalent Merlin Figure, a mad or evil false priest, presides. His eventual triumph over the charlatan becomes a ritual feat, a besting of the powers of darkness."[15]

Though the grail patterns can be overemphasized (the Temple of the Holy Grail, for example, was the Hotel Primrose in the *Black Mask* original version), Hammett seems to have intentionally highlighted them in *The Dain Curse*. A point-to-point correspondence could be made between Fitzstephan and an "ambivalent Merlin," or Gabrielle and Guinevere, or the Op and Lancelot. More important is the emotional resonance and cultural familiarity that readers bring to such patterns once revealed. *The Dain Curse* succeeds despite the gaps between the stories because the familiar quest beckons on. Readers understand that the temptation and affirmation of the hero's "character" will be more important than verisimilitude. This Op is not very hard-boiled. His nobility, Layman notes, "is emphasized once again, perhaps more dramatically than before, by his vulnerability."[16] His knighthood becomes clear when Upton and Ruppert are revealed as members of the round-table gone bad. His refusal to frame the Finks for Dr. Riese's murder, something he did without a second thought in "The Scorched Face," emphasizes that he is again in chivalric form. This makes him a suitable repository for Gabrielle's confession that she is still a virgin, despite sexual relations with three men. That he resists the temptation of the easy solution in the first section, the lure of mysticism in the second, and the suspicion of his Guinevere in the third, permits the Op to dispel the "curse" that afflicts Gabrielle.

Gabrielle's "disenchantment" depends on the Op's commitment to his code. Of this he is reminded when Mickey Linehan says, "I ought to tell her what happened to that poor girl [Dinah Brand] up in Poisonville that got so she thought she could trust you." The Op keeps Gabrielle at an emotional arms's length:

I said: "I'm twice your age sister; an old man. I'm damned if I'll make a chump of myself by telling you why I did it, why it was neither revolting or disgusting, why I'd do it again and be glad of the chance."
She jumped out of her chair, her eyes round and dark, her mouth trembling. "You mean—?"
"I don't mean anything that I'll admit," I said; "and if you're going to parade around with that robe hanging open you're going to get yourself some bronchitis."

Gabrielle does not "offer" herself to the Op, as some commentators believe, and he turns down the chance to exploit her, as his code requires (*DC*, 178).

Gabrielle's restoration required changes in her original physiognomy, a fact pointed out by Hammett's editor, who said she looked like a monkey for most of the book. It became a point of contention between Block, who did not understand the mythic level, and Hammett, who argued in a letter of 30 March 1929 that he had given Gabrielle *his own* anatomical details: he added that if Block found the details so terrible, he should go ahead and fix them himself.

Hammett did oblige his editor's request that he write transitional material for the gaps between the original stories, although he conceded that "the dingus is still undoubtedly rather complicated." Then there was the violence, regarded differently at Knopf than at *Black Mask*. "We have thought too that the violence is piled on a bit too thick," wrote Block, "and that cutting out one or two of the less important killings would do away with the danger of surfeiting the reader." Hammett eliminated one murder, but later said the novel was "still rather full of slaughter."

Reaction to *The Dain Curse*

The initial sales of *The Dain Curse* were substantially better than those of *Red Harvest*. It appeared on 19 July 1929 and sold 5,000 copies by the end of the month. In the *Outlook and Independent* Walter Brooks wrote that there was "only one story of the kind better than this second book of Mr. Hammett's and that is his first book." The *New York Times* reviewed it favorably, and Will Cuppy said in the *Herald Tribune* that it had "really astonishing speed."[17]

Ernest Hemingway years later recounted his experience with the novel in *Death in the Afternoon:* "My eyes were too bad to read," he wrote, "and my wife was reading Dashiell Hammett's bloodiest to date, *The Dain Curse,* out loud. . . ." To prevent his children from overhearing the carnage, Hemingway said, his wife substituted " 'umpty-umped' for the words killed, cut the throat of, blew the brains out of, spattered about the room and so on."[18]

Later critics have not liked the novel. Philip Durham wrote that Hammett "traded a hard-boiled hero for a part-time sentimentalist, a character who could recognize in himself such emotions as might be acceptable in the traditional hard-boiled hero, but for Hammett it could mean only that his hero had grown old and soft. Long live the Op. He was ready for discard." Hammett's own view of *The Dain Curse* is complicated by what he felt was a half-finished quality to it. He barely got the page proofs before the novel appeared, and he complained to Block that "the first forty pages . . . were edited to hell (hurriedly for the dummy?) and the rest hardly at all. The result was that, having amiably accepted most of your changes in the first part, I had my hands full carrying them out in the remainder, trying to make it look all the work of the same writer."[19]

The Dain Curse has been called "a plateau, not an upward step" and "an essentially less interesting performance." The arguments against it usually follow those of crime specialist John Martin:

In this single Hammett novel the detective shot and stabbed one man to death, helped shoot another dead, was himself attacked with dagger, gun, chloroform and bomb, fought off a ghostly manifestation barehanded, wrestled with five women, cured a girl of narcotic addiction—and . . . was obligated to deal with one seduction, eight murders, a jewel robbery and a family curse.[20]

Some of the time and effort that Hammett might have spent clarifying his plot and reducing his cast, to say nothing of unifying the grail motifs, was of course spent policing details of the text. Perhaps he forgot the ambitious goals of his letter to Mrs. Knopf, or sensed that *The Maltese Falcon,* on which he was working, was so much better that it merited unbroken attention.

Chapter Four
The Falcon and The Key
The Maltese Falcon

In his 1934 introduction to *The Maltese Falcon* Dashiell Hammett wrote:

> If this book had been written with the help of an outline or notes or even a clearly defined plot-idea in my head I might now be able to say how it came to be written and why it took the shape it did, but all I can remember about its invention is that somewhere I had read of the peculiar rental agreement between Charles V and the Order of the Hospital of Saint John of Jerusalem, that in a short story called "The Whosis Kid" I had failed to make the most of a situation I liked, that in another called "The Gutting of Couffignal" I had been equally fortunate with an equally promising denouement, and that I thought I might have better luck with these two failures if I combined them with the Maltese lease in a longer story.

The hallmark of the best modern American novelists has been an ability to recognize in the themes and plots of early work those conflicts that can sustain even greater elaboration. Call it a sieving or a critical eye, in 1928 Dashiell Hammett had it.

Hammett had written two novels in two years, had rewritten his old stories, and he claimed to have 250,000 words—an amount equal to half of the Bible—available for publication. This work was at once recapitulative and boldly innovative. In 1925, before he wrote "The Big Knockover" and "$106,000 Blood Money" to train up to the length of the novel, he had written two stories that were good but not quite finished. In "The Whosis Kid" most of the action took place in the apartment of Inés Almad, an alluring foreigner who fled with the loot from a robbery. The Op was in her apartment when three former partners showed up. The "situation" that Hammett liked was the "apartment drama," in which the rising action was heightened by the physically confining space and mutual hostility of the characters. The tension built extraordinarily well while it

70

was submerged in the dialogue, but the climax had been an ineffectual spate of bullets.

Hammett had known the advantage of tempting the hero's code with a beautiful woman since "The Girl with the Silver Eyes." But in "The Gutting of Couffignal" he attempted to increase the tension by making the Op's surrender circumstantially plausible. It failed. The Op seemed so uninvolved with the temptress that he sacrificed little in adhering to his code. In *The Maltese Falcon* Hammett clarified the archetypal traits of this femme fatale—beauty, mutability, duplicity—and involved the detective with her romantically from the first to the last chapter.

The Maltese Falcon is also given impetus by Hammett's elaborations on "classical" mystery formulas and by the reality/illusion debate that he explored in *The Dain Curse.* The use of violence to move the plot is much reduced; there are three murders, only one of them onstage. There are, however, ten important deceptions and reversals, and the detective himself is a deceiver, whose code takes shape from a parable about self-deception at the novel's core.

The detective is a new incarnation. In *The Dain Curse* Hammett seemed stumped about his hero's evolution and fell back on pure chivalric code. The hero of *The Maltese Falcon* recurs to the hero of *Red Harvest* in some traits, but in a more important way, as Hammett noted, he is an idealized vision of independence and self-reliance:

Spade had no original. He is a dream man in the sense that he is what most of the private detectives I worked with would like to have been and what quite a few of them in their cockier moments thought they approached. For your private detective does not—or did not ten years ago when he was my colleague—want to be an erudite solver of riddles in the Sherlock Holmes manner; he wants to be a hard and shifty fellow, able to take care of himself in any situation, able to get the best of anybody he comes in contact with, whether criminal, innocent by-stander or client.[1]

Sam Spade is the hero who looks "rather pleasantly like a blond satan." From jaw to widow's peak, his face repeats a *V* motif. He is slope-shouldered, compact, and muscular, so that mien and physique together suggest an extroverted, physical man. His partner Miles Archer is a similar but less intelligent type. Their office is managed by Effie Perrine, a "lanky, sunburned girl" with a "shiny boyish face," who became Perry Mason's Della Street and every private eye's secretary afterward.

The action begins when Effie escorts into Spade's office a Miss Wonderly, really Brigid O'Shaughnessy: she asks Spade to rescue her sister from a hoodlum named Floyd Thursby, and she advances $200 for the work. Miles Archer walks in, sizes her up, and volunteers to do the job. A 2 a.m. call from the police informs Spade that Archer has been murdered. He taxis to the scene but declines to examine the body or answer questions. "I'll bury my dead," he says. He asks Effie to call Iva Archer with the news. At home Spade is questioned by policemen Polhaus and Dundy, who have learned that he was cuckolding his partner, which makes him a suspect. They also reveal that Thursby is dead.

Miss Wonderly disappears, and has changed her name to Miss LeBlanc when Spade finds her. She only confesses her real name in the first "apartment scene," a histrionic meld of confessions, tears, and innuendos that does not fool Spade. But he agrees to help her recover a "valuable object" for an additional $500.

At the office the next day Effie ushers in Joel Cairo, who also gives Spade a retainer to help him find the object, which he identifies as the Maltese falcon. He pulls a gun on Spade, is disarmed, but repeats the trick as he leaves—all to no avail. After his contact with Cairo a man begins to shadow Spade, necessitating elaborate dodges. Brigid will not divulge details about the quest for the falcon, but, like Princess Zhukovski, offers to buy Spade's trust with her body. This disturbs Spade, who arranges a meeting between Cairo and Brigid.

Waiting for Cairo, Spade tells Brigid the story of Flitcraft. It seems like idle conversation, but it is a parable explaining, indeed forecasting, Spade's behavior. When Cairo arrives, he trades sexual insults with Brigid (he is a homosexual) until Dundy and Polhaus appear again. The police threaten to jail all three. Only Spade's brilliant improvisation, in which he persuades Cairo to play a part, prevents their arrest. Dundy again accuses Spade of Archer's murder, and punches him on the way out. Drawing on his deepest reserve of discipline, Spade refrains from striking back, but after the police and Cairo leave, he flies into a rage. The scene ends with Spade and Brigid on the way to bed, but readers are warned away from assuming paramount importance for the love interest. Spade wakes before Brigid the next morning, and searches her apartment while she sleeps.

With a clue garnered the previous night, Spade finds the man shadowing him and says he wants to see "G." When he returns to his office, Spade has a call from G., who is Casper Gutman. The shadow, a "gunsel" or kept-boy named Wilmer, escorts Spade to see Gutman. Like Effie, Wilmer has passed into the archetypal library of the detective novel. From Gutman Spade learns more about the "black bird" and those who seek it;

he pretends to possess it and gives Gutman a dead-line for his participation in its recovery.

Fearing that Gutman will kill her, Brigid goes into hiding. When Spade applies himself to tracking her down, he can find no clues except a newspaper clipping about a ship due from Hong Kong called *La Paloma*. When Gutman calls and opts in, Spade learns the entire story of the falcon. Hammett embellished the history of the icon's later travels, but the data on the Hospitalers of Saint John is basically correct. They were a religious order in the Middle Ages, located on the Isle of Rhodes, and charged with providing lodging and care for pilgrims on the way to Jerusalem. They built up tremendous wealth between 1300 and the early 1500s, but were displaced by Suleiman the Magnificent and his Turkish armies in 1523. They wandered until 1530, when they gained the patronage of Charles V, who gave them four islands, including Malta (not three, as Gutman says). The actual Hospitalers were displeased by the barren islands and savage inhabitants, but delighted that the only required tribute was "simple presentation of a yearly falcon on All-Saints Day."[2] Initially they gave a live bird, but as their wealth grew they substituted jewel-encrusted statuettes.

At the finish of the history, Spade passes out—Gutman had drugged him. On waking, he finds Gutman, Wilmer, and Cairo gone. When he goes to search Cairo's room, he finds another clue leading to *La Paloma*, but is prevented from pursuing it by appointments with Polhaus and the district attorney. Then as Spade and Effie discuss the day's events at the office, Captain Jacobi of *La Paloma* enters, carrying the wrapped falcon, and falls dead at their feet.

Spade instructs Effie to phone the police while he hides the falcon. He tries to contact Gutman, but the criminals conspire to send him on a wild goose chase. Since Brigid participates in the deception, Spade is suspicious when she appears outside his door that evening. Gutman, Cairo, and Wilmer are waiting upstairs; Spade knows he is trapped. He accepts $10,000 to deliver the falcon, but insists that a "fall-guy" be given to the police for the murders. First he suggests Wilmer, then Cairo. Gutman suggests Brigid and attempts to impeach her by suggesting that she stole one of the ten $1,000 bills that she has been holding for Spade. When this ploy fails, Gutman and Cairo agree to make Wilmer the fall guy.

As dawn approaches, Spade phones Effie to retrieve and deliver the falcon. Unwrapped, it turns out to be a worthless imitation; Gutman asks for his money back, and Spade gives him all but $1,000, which he later turns over to the police. The irrepressible Gutman decides to continue his search, and Cairo joins him. As they leave Spade alerts Polhaus and Dundy, but before the criminals can be arrested Wilmer kills Gutman. Spade urges Brigid to tell all before the police arrive. She confesses to conspiring to get the falcon, but denies involvement in Archer's murder. However all of the evidence points to her. "Miles hadn't many brains," says Spade, " . . . but he'd have gone up [the alley] with you, angel, if he was sure nobody else was up there."[3] When Brigid confesses, she attempts to force Spade's loyalty by invoking their love. In the stunning climax, Spade says that "maybe you love me and maybe I love you" but that he "won't play the sap for her." He enumerates seven reasons why, then turns her over to Polhaus and Dundy.

The novel ends on a melancholic note the next morning as Effie Perrine will have nothing to do with Spade because he has betrayed the cause of true love. Iva Archer waits outside, however, and when Effie ushers her in Spade shudders and seems resigned to an emotional wasteland.

The Importance of Flitcraft

The rightness of the ending, as well as an understanding of Spade's earlier actions, rest on the story that he told about Flitcraft. Occurring before he goes to bed with Brigid, the parable's structural position is like that of the dream sequence in *Red Harvest* or the fight with the ghost in *The Dain Curse*. But thematically it is better integrated. Flitcraft is a reinterpretation of the character Norman Ashcraft in "The Golden Horseshoe," and like other aspects of the novel he has become immortal—there are probability statistics in the insurance business known as *Flitcraft Reports.* In Hammett's first treatment, Ashcraft resents his wife's wealth and wants to prove that he can support himself independently. He moves to America, leads a scruffy life, and is in a sense reincarnated in the criminal Ed Bohannon. The fantasy of an enjoyably disreputable life available beyond the marital confines is a strong and attractive aspect of the earlier story.

In Hammett's reworking, Flitcraft is a real estate agent who leaves his office for lunch one noon and never returns. He passes a construction site and "a beam or something fell eight or ten stories down and smacked the sidewalk alongside him." Suddenly Flitcraft's eyes opened: "He felt like somebody had taken the lid off life and let him look at the works." Life was not a "clean, orderly, sane, responsible affair," he saw rather that "men died at haphazard like that, and lived only while blind chance spared them." According to Spade, "What disturbed him was the discovery that in sensibly ordering his affairs he had got out of step and not into step, with life. He said he knew before he had gone twenty feet from the fallen beam that he would never know peace again until he had adjusted himself to this new glimpse of life. . . . Life could be ended for him at random by a falling beam: he would change his life at random by simply going away."

This naturalistic conception of the universe leads Flitcraft to wander for several years, eventually marrying a woman similar to his first wife and replicating his old circumstances. Spade "always liked" this part of the story, which shows the primacy of the adaptive response: "I don't think he even knew he had settled back naturally into the same groove he had jumped out of in Tacoma. . . . He adjusted himself to beams falling, and then no more of them fell and he adjusted himself to them not falling" (*MF*, 65–67).

The moral, which Brigid misses, lies at the level of Spade's ironic appreciation rather than in Flitcraft's insight into the nature of the universe. The universe may be material and organized by chance, one may die any second; but such an insight, as Flitcraft demonstrates, does not mean that randomness constitutes a way of life. Man is above all adaptive and habitual, traits not only rationally intelligible but rather predictable. Information keeps crystallizing in a chaotic universe. Spade, for example, has found Flitcraft. Herein lies the basic irony that pervades Spade's outlook: the world may not operate rationally, but rationality is the best net with which to go hunting. The chance event—the falling beam—drives men away from cover and adaptive responses for a short time.

In telling Brigid this, Spade is explaining that his code is primary for him. It is the best adaptive response to the world in which he lives, a version of James Wright's advice to Hammett back in 1915. Spade has seen the potency of chance events—and love might be numbered among them—and he understands their relation to the patterns. Were Brigid at all perceptive about this story, she would see that each time she deceives him, Spade becomes more certain of her pattern. His "wild and unpredictable monkey-wrenches" repeatedly unseat her from romantic postures and reveal her fundamental avarice. But the uncomprehending Brigid only says "How perfectly fascinating" at the end of the Flitcraft story.

The Moral Climate of *The Maltese Falcon*

Hammett's most extraordinary fictional feat is the embodiment of this world view in the character of Sam Spade. Spade is a continuation of that interest, which Hammett expressed in *The Dain Curse*, in the deceptions that veil reality. Reality is Spade's psychological fulcrum, and yet he is more perfectly than the Op a knight of the detective code. But readers perceive him as flawed, cruel, and human, rather than as the holder of God-like powers. Hammett masks his character's power primarily by eliminating the first-person narrator, whose intimacy with the reader revealed his minor infidelities to the code and implied that he discussed his cases, a weakness alien to the entirely private personality of Spade. With a third-person point of view, the hero's person becomes more distant and independent. In addition, Hammett made Spade's code an innovation on the generic standard, a new version that allows him not only deception, but the pleasures of adultery and the rewards of betrayal. Such variations are the key mode of creativity in popular literature, allowing readers to enjoy generically or conventionally forbidden desires.

Yet Spade's code is only one of three moral climates. The reader is exposed equally to the worlds of the police and of the criminals, whose ethos Brigid shares. The exact distinctions between these worlds are blurred, and the reality/illusion question makes it clear that both Spade and the reader function, when they judge, on the basis of only some of the facts. More facts may be produced by "heaving a wild and unpredictable monkey-wrench into the works," as Spade says, but he never forgets that his facts, once linked, are still a construction of reality. As he tells his lawyer of Iva Archer's alibi, "I don't believe it or disbelieve it. . . . I don't know a damned thing about it." What counts, he explains, is that it seems "to click with most of the known facts" and "ought to hold" (*MF*, 120). Spade operates on this view of reality for the entire novel; at its end he refuses to tell Brigid whether he would have acted differently had the falcon been real and they shared its wealth.

Hammett had a bit of fun articulating Spade's world view: when Flitcraft assumes his new existence, he changes his name to Charles Pierce, a variation on Charles Sanders Peirce, the nineteenth-century American philosopher who wrote extensively about chance and probability.[4] Peirce also identified a logical process between induction and deduction called "abduction," in which the investigator accepts an event as having happened, then imagines the state of affairs that produced the situation. Its common use in detective fiction, as Hammett saw, reinforced the role of the detective as the author of reality.

The method is apropos, since the characters with whom Spade must deal live according to illusions. Most of them are greedy; they want the falcon. For some, such as Gutman, this greed is overlain with the illusion of personal quest. Others, such as Brigid, believe the world is made up of "saps," who can be manipulated by their sexual desires. All such illusions are, on the allegoric level, symbolic sins. Those of Joel Cairo, the effete criminal, and Wilmer, the homosexual gunman, have become less obvious as their characters became more stereotyped. Rhea Gutman's self-abuse is a continuation of Gabrielle Leggett's morbid self-destruction. Miles Archer, with his sartorial self-confidence, represents a traditional pride, while Effie Perrine, with her romantic conception of love, is a more simply deluded, but nonetheless erring, variation on a generic norm.

Reasoning as he does by abduction, Spade maintains his personal distance on these characters until he abduces (authors) their formative situations. He understands that everyone lives in his illusions, so he believes nothing, trusts no one, and rejects real emotional contact. Critic Bernard Schopen points out that Gutman, Cairo, Wilmer, and Brigid are moral primitives, who "create those illusions which assist them in their rapacious pursuits."[5] Most affective are those of Brigid, whose continual lies and deceptions readers excuse as long as she feigns inchoate personal emotions—claiming thus an emotional sanctity. This implication of mystery makes her character far more interesting than those of Jeanne Delano in "The Girl with the Silver Eyes" or the princess in "The Gutting of Couffignal." Yet it is the reader, not Spade, that she seduces with her sentiments. Spade merely speaks the lingua franca of each character's illusion and avoids the fate of "saps" like Archer and Thursby, who are induced to participate.

The abductive method is complicated by those properties of the formal mystery that Hammett appropriated for the structure of *The Maltese Falcon.* He had been experimenting with analytic detection in *The Dain Curse,* and was fond of the trail of false clues that he used in "The Tenth Clew." The ten deceptions in *The Maltese Falcon*, according to George Thompson, begin with Brigid's representation of herself as Miss Wonderly and her portrayal of Thursby as Archer's killer. The third is Dundy's opinion that Spade murdered Archer, a view supported by new information about Spade's affair with Iva and testimony from Archer's brother. If the reader is suspicious of Spade at this point, Hammett has successfully involved him in the skeptical world view that is Spade's *modus operandi,* and the point of the Flitcraft parable. The fourth deception is Brigid's story connecting herself and Thursby to the falcon, for she says that she is the victim of the latter's greed. Later, the implication in her disappearance is that she has become the victim of foul play. The sixth deception occurs when she calls Spade for help, the seventh when the police theorize that Thursby's death is the result of underworld warfare. The wild goose chase to Burlingame is the eighth false clue, and the ninth is the $1,000 bill that Gutman palms in the final showdown. That the falcon itself is a worthless phony is the tenth and paramount deception. It suddenly illuminates the moral and spiritual emptiness of the co-conspirators, and ironically belittles their quest. It also links the nine previous deceptions in one paramount symbol of the three plot elements—the investigation of Archer's death, the mystery of the falcon, and the romance between Spade and Brigid.

The Flitcraft parable itself shines through the ten plot deceptions to illuminate the grail/quest structure in a new light. When the grail is found to be worthless, the implication is that the emotion Brigid generates is a "falling beam," discredited by her greed. But it is also true that while they seek it, the grail holds Spade and Brigid together. It represents the emptiness of sentimental emotion, but its pursuit is, paradoxically, an adaptive response, a confirming, stabilizing influence in Western society. But it no longer provides a "solution." Like so many American writers of the late twenties, Hammett sees continual emotional improvisation as the only answer. The fact that Flitcraft's life is Hammett's personal meditation on what he himself should do next makes the symbol extraordinarily compelling.

The Women in Spade's Life

There are only four women in the novel. Rhea Gutman has been discussed. The others, as Hammett indicates in "Three Women," serve in one sense as the "fates." They ask questions, represent mysteries, and possess occult powers; Spade depends particularly on Effie's "female intuition." But they are also prosaic "fates," typifying three possibilities for Spade. Effie is a kind of "office wife," who is capable, dependable, and part of a team. Spade's physical intimacies with her are uncharged, innocent as a small boy's bedtime hug in the kitchen. It is appropriate that the falcon should come to Effie and Spade, because they function psychologically as a nuclear family, and one of the subliminal features of popular entertainment is the reinforcement of tradition.

The falcon must be exposed as a fake in the presence of the second woman, Brigid, whose romantic outlook and effusive sexuality the reinforcing function rejects. Brigid's name signifies, like Gabrielle Leggett's, a touch of foreignness. As Miss Le Blanc, she recalls Blanchfleur, who nearly diverted Sir Galahad from his quest for the grail. Her beauty and sexual intensity are only one aspect of this "loathly lady"; her dark side is ingrown with lies and deceit. "I always lie," she confesses to Spade, in a scene that is her analogue to the Flitcraft parable. Although she seems to promise Spade an existence of mutual intensities, Brigid is a type not capable of bonding emotions. Iva Archer falls between Effie and Brigid. Like Myrtle Jennison in *Red Harvest,* she serves as a cautionary example of the wages of sin: Spade's inclination is to pull the covers over her and to say "Thank you" when he is done. Yet she is Spade's lot when the novel ends, and there is something so reduced, petty, and limited in her character that it makes Spade shiver. To have Iva is to become Archer, to cuckold oneself. The irony the reader feels is that experienced when a stolen pleasure becomes a gift of ennui.

The three women are also configured to be sexually significant. As psychiatrists have pointed out, the deaths of Archer and Thursby leave Spade in possession of two women who were formerly attached to other men. There is a "fear of Oedipal victory" attached to this, of which overmuch can be made, but it undoubtedly lends tension to the plot. The sexual problem gains a third element when two of the women contrast with Effie, the "desexualized daytime mother."[6] Hammett's scheme of sexual temptation became a convention of detective fiction. Although usually there are two women, a blonde and a brunette, the detective must find the more beautiful woman guilty. He is compelled to arrest her, or in the brutal world of Micky Spillane to destroy her. "The particular terms of this sacrifice suggest the marked tendency of American fiction to depict women as potentially destructive," notes George Grella.[7] Yet artists of Hammett's rank, such as Chandler and Macdonald, have found the convention useful to more humane themes (see *The Little Sister*).

The archetype itself dates back to the Middle Ages; in pure form she is called the succubus. Heroes of the early grail romances, such as Percival, were afflicted by succubi. When Hammett calls upon this peril, however, the effect is more subtle than in a morality drama because the novel has realistic and romantic levels too. These put the love relationship in higher relief than the quest or the question of who killed Miles Archer. Readers forget that Spade has told Brigid the story of Flitcraft, which he conceives as a warning, for he concludes, " 'You don't have to trust me, anyhow, as long as you can persuade me to trust you.' " They forget that Brigid thinks she seduces Spade by warning "I am a liar. I have always been a liar."

The tension resulting from their liaison highlights the romance element in the crucial scene. The exchange of secrets seems to lock them together. Brigid has been forewarned about Spade, but she stays because, like Dinah Brand, she is hypnotized by treasure. Spade keeps close to Brigid, even when she gives him false leads and deliberately loses him, because he cannot believe that he will be as naive as Archer when Brigid reveals her ultimate allure to him.

And indeed he is not. After Spade's muscles stand out "like wales," he goes on to enumerate the reasons why he must turn her in. In the ritual of enumeration, the archetype is being summoned to unite the romantic, realistic, and allegoric levels. Surrender to emotion means surrender of self-conception, and ultimately death. "I won't because all of me wants to—wants to say to hell with the consequences and do it—and because—God damn you—you counted on that with me the same as you counted on that with the others," says Spade. To succumb is to be mortal, to see one's individuality mocked by the engulfing pattern of one's inferiors. But to suppress the almost chemical certainty of lust is to free oneself from commonness and obtain a measure of immortality. Consummation would bring a shattering confrontation with Spade's own inner emptiness and isolation—the function of "reason" here is to inform the hero that intimacy is death, which allows the mythic to predominate.

The ultimate horror that the femme fatal embodies changes with the prevailing malaise of the age. To be meaningful her threat of death through sexuality must have a current equivalent, a clear representation of death-in-life. Hammett's triumph in *The Maltese Falcon* is the way in which he develops the psychological meaning at the archetype's core on a basis of a coherent and credible intimacy. Spade's decision stuns readers because it suddenly reclaims the power that belongs to the archetypal, transcending the sentimentality with which authors usually afflict their heroes.

The Technique of *The Maltese Falcon*

The Maltese Falcon is Dashiell Hammett's most technically adept novel. Sustaining breakneck speed through the intricacies that confront Spade is no slight accomplishment. More than usual Hammett's prose has a clipped, elided quality that gestures matter-of-factly to the world under the reader's nose. The similarity of this style and that of Hemingway's early work is often noted, though Hemingway's terseness points to an interior world of complex, inexpressible emotions that the reader is meant to perceive.

The terseness of *The Maltese Falcon* owes not to complexity of perception, but to each word's function as an engine of plot. And few words move the action as rapidly as those in the characters' speeches. The entire novel, William Nolan writes, "is basically a series of brilliant dialogues, set in motion and bolstered by offstage events."[8] Hammett elaborates a distinct conversational style for each character on his or her first appearance. Spade's habitual use of "Sweetheart," "Darling," and "Angel" with women establishes his character and emotional invulnerability at the outset. Just as distinctive is Brigid's first stammering, truncated line: "She swallowed and said hurriedly: 'Could you—? I thought—I—that is—' " She breaks off questions and statements before they are complete, as if overwhelmed by emotion, when she is concealing the facts. She draws her listeners into answers to incomplete questions. Gutman, Effie, Iva, Dundy, Polhaus, and Cairo have comparable conversational signatures.

Hammett also structured his characters and their moods by noting their important habits. In Sam Spade's case these became ritual, a technique that Hammett undoubtedly did notice in Hemingway's work. Most famous is Spade's habit of rolling, rerolling, lighting, and extinguishing his own Bull Durham cigarettes, according to the tenor of the talk or his own thoughts. Hammett introduces the reader to this ceremony in the first pages, after Spade learns of Archer's murder:

> Spade's thick fingers made a cigarette with deliberate care, sifting a measured quantity of tan flakes down into the curved paper, spreading the flakes slightly so that they lay equal at the ends with a slight depression in the middle, thumbs rolling the paper's inner edge down and up under the outer edge as forefingers pressed it over, thumbs and fingers sliding to the paper's cylinder ends to hold it even while tongue licked the flap, left forefinger and thumb pinching their end while right forefinger and thumb smoothed the damp seam, right forefinger and thumb twisting their end and lifting the other to Spade's mouth. (*MF*, 11–12)

The making of the cigarette, its absence, or a pause in its construction are all intended to intimate Spade's inner state. There may be sexual symbolism in the cigarette's shape, but it is more important that the ritual indicates an order beyond articulation—the detective code. Hammett changed the details of the novel in this direction in its final draft. Nolan notes, for instance, the substitution of "They shook hands ceremoniously" for "They shook hands with marked formality."[9]

Hammett refined the detective novel's handling of stereotypic characterization in *The Maltese Falcon*. Moved by their romantic interest in him, most readers forget the opening description of Spade:

> Sam Spade's jaw was long and bony, his chin a jutting V under the more flexible V of his mouth. His nostrils curved back to make another, smaller V. His yellow-grey eyes were horizontal. The V motif was picked up again by the

thickish brows rising outward . . . and his pale brown hair grew down—from rather high flat temples—in a point on his forehead. He looked rather pleasantly like a blond satan. (*MF, 3*)

This is wit carried almost to parody, an impossible face. No one forgets the portrait of Casper Gutman, however, which harks back to Vasilije Djudakovich in "This King Business":

The fat man was flabbily fat with bulbous pink cheeks and lips and chins and neck, with a great soft egg of a belly that was all his torso, and pendant cones for arms and legs. As he advanced to meet Spade all his bulbs rose and shook and fell separately with each step, in the manner of clustered soap-bubbles not yet released from the pipe through which they had been blown. (*MF, 108*)

Despite his embroidery of the characters, Hammett claimed to have had real models in mind. "I followed Gutman's original in Washington," he said, "and I never remember shadowing a man who bored me so much. He was not after a jeweled falcon, of course." Hammett said "Brigid was based, in part, on a woman who came in to Pinkerton's to hire an operative to discharge her housekeeper." Nolan adds that Brigid was based also on Peggy O'Toole, the advertising artist with whom Hammett shared an office at Samuels's in San Francisco. "The Cairo character I picked up on a forgery charge in 1920," said Hammett. "Effie, the good girl, once asked me to go into the narcotic smuggling business with her in San Diego. Wilmer, the gunman was picked up in Stockton, California, a neat small smooth-faced quiet boy of perhaps twenty-one. He was serenely proud of the name the paper gave him—The Midget Bandit." He was also the character on whom Hammett had based his story "Itchy."[10]

The most notable departure from Hammett's preceding work is the lack of violence in *The Maltese Falcon*. Only one character, Captain Jacobi of *La Paloma,* dies onstage, and he is shot earlier offstage. The deaths of Archer and Thursby occur between the moments of the present action. Nor is the reader subjected to the graphic descriptions of bullet and dagger holes that Hammett had prized as recently as *The Dain Curse*. Violence is present, but psychological. An oppressing sense of closure brackets every meeting and conversation, creating a climate of emotional claustrophobia that is the diminutive of the threat of the larger world. In other words, the apartment scenes imply by their interior concentration a great external threat. As the settings increasingly become interiors, Hammett connotes more psychological peril than he could in pages of graphic violence.

Violence becomes more personal as the characters become more familiar, until after the final scene between Spade and Brigid the reader feels that intimacy is its most fecund soil. Capped on the symbolic level by the falcon, this psychological violence raises the novel far above its genre.

The Debate on the Ending

The culmination of the tension is the confrontation between Sam and Brigid, the nature and satisfactoriness of which has been debated for some twenty years now. At first there was some contention that the end of the novel was flawed. William Kenney argued that,

The emotional climax of the novel is surely the scene in which Spade tells Brigid of his intention to turn her over to the police. Yet this scene grows out of what has been only a minor element in the plot, the murder of Miles Archer. The novel's main action, the quest for the falcon, reaches its climax with the discovery that the bird is not genuine. There is then a structural division in the final episodes of the novel, giving the scene between Spade and Brigid, excellent as it is in itself, almost the air of an afterthought.

Since that time, several scholars have argued that the novel achieves its final coherence in the symbol of the falcon. One of Hammett's heirs, Ross Macdonald, voiced this view: "The black bird," he wrote, "is hollow, worthless. The reality behind appearance is a treacherous vacuum. . . . The bird's lack of value implies Hammett's final comment on the inadequacy and superficiality of Spade's life and ours. If only his bitterly inarticulate struggle for self-realization were itself more fully realized . . . Sam Spade could have become a great, indigenous tragic figure. . . . I think *The Maltese Falcon* . . . is tragedy of a new kind, deadpan tragedy." The discovery that the falcon is a fake, most scholars now agree, implies a side to the Spade-O'Shaughnessy relationship that could only be resolved in a tandem climax.[11]

The discovery of the bogus falcon should focus readers' attention on the nature of the novel's emotional world. The emotional middle distance in which Spade operates has made it difficult to ascertain his real feelings. Brigid is a habitual liar, and Hammett allows Effie to put in a word for romantic love on the last page. Few critics are willing to assert that Sam is in love with Brigid, notes George Thompson, who boldly suggests "that Hammett means us to take their relationship seriously." He argues that Hammett portrayed "a subtle rendering of Spade's growing personal anguish" in the final scene by means of the grammatical modifiers: "Spade said *tenderly*: "You angel! Well, if you get a good break you'll be out of San Quentin in twenty years. . . . He was *pale.* He said *tenderly*: "I hope to God they don't hang you, precious, by that sweet neck." Thompson argues that the lines that follow may "sound like clichés now" but that they "were a first in the 1930s, and unless our own cynicism gets in the way, what comes through here is the strength of his feeling for her."[12]

But there are as many grammatical qualifiers on the other side of the argument. Spade "smiled wolfishly," "laughed harshly," "demanded in a low, impatient voice," and "slapped her shoulder" in this scene. Most commentators agree that Spade, with great emotional effort, maintains his distance from Brigid. The issue has become: how are readers finally to judge Spade's character?

Among those sympathetic to Spade as a realistic character (though not as literally inclined as Thompson), William Nolan's argument is perhaps the most cogent:

> It would be a mistake to judge Spade as "unscrupulous" and "heartless." In the climactic sequence in which he finally turns Brigid over to the police he reveals the emotions of a man whose heart is with the woman, but whose code forbids his accepting her. Spade knows that he cannot continue to function if he breaks his personal code and goes off with Brigid—even while he admits that Miles Archer was "a louse" and that the agency is better off without him. Sam can sleep with Iva, the dead man's wife; he can bed down with his secretary (" . . . his hand on her hip . . . 'Don't touch me now—not now.' ") and he can spend the night with Brigid, but he must never make a permanent alliance with any of them, the good or the evil.[13]

Yet to concede that Spade acts on his code in the final scene is to admit the primacy of the code in the novel. In Robert Edenbaum's brilliant interpretation, he notes that "in the last pages of the novel . . . the reader (and Brigid O'Shaughnessy) discovers that he (and she) has been duped all along," for Spade has known from the moment he saw Archer's body that Brigid was the murderer. "Spade himself then is the one person who holds the central piece of information," writes Edenbaum; "he is the one person who knows everything, for Brigid does not know that he knows. And though Spade is no murderer, Brigid O'Shaughnessy is his victim." Edenbaum contends that "Brigid . . . is the manipulated, the deceived, the unpredictable, finally, in a very real sense, the victim." In Edenbaum's view the course of the action is "the demolition of sentiment" through the "all but passionless figure of Spade." The key to this interpretation is Edenbaum's insight that Spade is a kind of "daemonic agent," a vehicle of allegoric impulse. Those who try to redeem the sentimental level of the action have missed the point, says Edenbaum. They say "You're right, you're right, but couldn't you better have been wrong? As Hammett made sufficiently clear . . . in the final confrontation with Brigid, exactly the point about Spade . . . is that he could not have."[14]

This interpretation gains rather than loses plausibility when considered in tandem with the final scene, in which Spade sits in his office and shivers at the prospect of meeting Iva. There is always at the end of the hard-boiled detective novel a moment of depression, when the detective reflects on the loss of a girl friend or colleague. But usually the tone implies that, rather than being defeated, he is essentially alone. This scene is Hammett's echo of that convention, but it also enforces the allegoric level that Edenbaum points out. By its nature allegory works to maintain a cultural consensus about the nature of reality and the exigency of morality. There must be human costs, and neither allegory nor its popular derivations can deny this without losing their deeper appeal. Spade's loss of Brigid and dismissal by Effie show this cost. Brigid's fate would not surprise anyone who had read "Nelson Redline," Hammett's short story of 1924. In it he wrote that people "who refuse to—or for one reason or another are unable to—conduct themselves in accordance with the accepted rules—no matter how strong their justification may be, or how foolish the rules—have to be put outside." Spade must be "put outside" by Effie, in part because he put Brigid outside.

Hammett Finds Success

Hammett knew as he was writing that *The Maltese Falcon* was good work, and he was thinking about how to convert it to other salable forms. He needed money to finance his planned move to New York City. On 16 June 1929 he wrote to Block, his editor at Knopf:

> I started THE MALTESE FALCON on its way to you by express last Friday, the fourteenth. I'm fairly confident that it is by far the best thing I've done so far, and I hope you'll think so too.
>
> Though I hadn't anything of the sort in mind while doing it, I think now that it could very easily be turned into a play. Will you let me know if you agree with me? I wouldn't take a chance of trying to adapt it myself, but will try to get the help of somebody who knows the theatre.

Another thing: if you use THE FALCON will you go a little easy on the editing? While I wouldn't go to the stake in defense of my system of punctuation, I do rather like it and I think it goes with my system of sentence structure.[15]

The major problem that Hammett had with Block (and with his editor at *Black Mask*) was with the sex in the story. In 1929 magazines and publishing houses exercised stringent self-censorship. Cap Shaw had cut some of the sexual banter between Brigid and Joel Cairo, such as her line "The one you couldn't make," but Hammett restored it for Knopf, and Block let it stand. Shaw changed Spade's baiting of Wilmer—"How long have you been off the gooseberry lay?"—to "How long have you been off the lay?" making it more explicit in the process, he supposed, of purging the homoeroticism. But he left in "gunsel" (a boy kept by a homosexual), assuming that it meant gunman, as millions have continued to believe. The words "hell" and "damn" were permitted in both the magazine and book forms, but the all-American expletive was forbidden. Hammett got around that with the construction "The boy spoke two words, the first a short guttural verb, the second 'you.'" However, Block objected to the direct indications at the end of chapter 9 and at the beginning of chapter 10 that Sam and Brigid sleep together. Knopf's Borzoi series put itself above prurient interest. Hammett answered this criticism in a letter:

Dear Mr. Block:
I'm glad you like THE MALTESE FALCON. I'm sorry you think the to-bed and the homosexual parts of it should be changed. I should like to leave them as they are, especially since you say they "would be all right perhaps in an ordinary novel." It seems to me that the only thing that can be said against their use in a detective novel is that nobody has tried it yet. I'd like to try it.[16]

Fearful of offending readers of the series, Block held out for the changes. He was lucky that Hammett was becoming famous and was busy moving. On 31 August Hammett wrote: "OK—go ahead and change them. I don't imagine a few words difference will matter greatly, and anyway, I'll soon be on hand to do in person whatever crying is necessary."

Unlike his previous novels, *The Maltese Falcon* was immediately popular. Cap. Shaw had hyped the *Black Mask* serialization with his personal testimony—"In all of my experience I have never encountered a story as intense, as gripping or as powerful as this one . . . ," and the reviewers who had been following Hammett since *Red Harvest* could not praise it enough.[17] Walter Brooks of the *Outlook and Independent* wrote, "This is not only probably the best detective story we have ever read, it is an exceedingly well-written novel." Will Cuppy wrote in the *New York Herald Tribune* that "it would not surprise us one whit if Mr. Hammett turned out to be the Great American mystery writer." Alexander Woollcott thought the novel "the best detective story America has yet produced." Another critic said "the writing is better than Hemingway."[18]

Hammett also gained the intellectual respect that he had sought since his earlier contributions to the *Smart Set*. The *New Republic* noted that *The Maltese Falcon* was "not the tawdry gum-shoeing of the ten-cent magazine. It is the genuine presence of the myth." The aristocratic *Town & Country* devoted 1,500 words of effusive praise to the novel.

It is likely that the praise Hammett appreciated most came from fellow writers. Herbert Asbury, a reviewer, praised the novel. Hammett responded: "I can't tell you how pleased I was with your verdict on "The Maltese Falcon." It's the first thing I've done that was—regardless of what faults it had—the best work I was capable of at the time I was doing it."

The verdict that this is Hammett's best work has not changed. Raymond Chandler wrote that "*The Maltese Falcon* may or may not be a work of genius, but an art which is capable of it is not 'by hypothesis' incapable of anything. Once a detective story can be as good as this, only the pedants will deny that it *could* be even better." And Ross Macdonald noted "its astonishing imaginative energy persisting undiminished after more than a third of a century." *The Maltese Falcon* broke the barriers of the genre; it was, and is, a work of art.[19]

The Glass Key

The writing of *The Glass Key* taxed Dashiell Hammett's creative powers and personal stamina—it was the fourth novel that he published in a thirty-two month stretch between November 1927 and June 1930. The novel began appearing in *Black Mask* in March 1930, just a few months before Hammett separated from his family and moved to the big world of New York. Unlike the sudden burst of *The Maltese Falcon* this manuscript progressed slowly. When publisher Alfred Knopf asked after it, Hammett wrote back, " 'The Glass Key' is coming along slowly but not badly. I shan't leave to New York next week as I had expected but shall be there in any event by the first of October." But to a friend Hammett confided that he had been "held back thus far by laziness, drunkenness and illness."[20]

Hammett felt that the finished book was his best work, nonetheless, because "the clues were nicely placed . . . although nobody seemed to see them." Reviewers were less sanguine. David T. Bazelon, writing for *Commentary,* thought that Hammett had attempted a conventional novel, in which characters act for reasons of loyalty, passion, or power. But even on those generous grounds, he found the novel unsatisfactory: "We never know whether [the] motive in solving the murder is loyalty, job-doing or love." Other critics wrote that the novel was "Hammett's least satisfactory," and that the hero was "mechanical and his emotions were not there."[21]

The Glass Key represents some falling off from the dramatic tension and vivid characterization of *The Maltese Falcon,* but most of the critical panning of the novel can be laid to Hammett's disappointment of generic expectations. He did not do the same thing twice in his major work. It would have been difficult to improve on the tight plot, quick-sketch characters, and cascading tension of *The Maltese Falcon;* that was the end of one line of Hammett's development. Returning to his earlier, more "serious" agenda, he decided that a looser plot struture would permit more development of human conflicts, especially the question of love. In place of his former devices, he would rely on the tension inherent in "tough guy" fiction, and the crispness created by Hemingway's elliptic technique and Dos Passos's realm. The "white space" that Hemingway advocated becomes, in *The Glass Key,* the use of such clues as letters, notes, and phone calls, without an explanatory context. Hammett's use of newspaper clippings as parts of the plot indicates a generally unnoticed debt to realism. Most puzzling for his audience was that Hammett dared to demand close reading.

The World of "Tough Guy" Fiction

The setting of *The Glass Key* is Poisonville on a larger scale. Though the physical locale is not specified, the moral milieu harks back to Hammett's first novel—a vista of endemic greed, where corrupt police and politicians operate under the protection of a businessman-powerbroker who is at war with a bootlegger. The power matrix is just as corrupt, but Hammett portrays it from the inside this time. Always balancing his critiques, Hammett gives this city a few early traces of humanity. The boss provides for a foot soldier's pregnant wife and child while he is in jail, and Ned Beaumont protects the innocent Opal from the enquiries of the corrupt district attorney. But afterward Hammett paints a dark picture of society. Senator Henry, the aristocrat of the novel, is a megalomaniac, like Old

Elihu, who sees his inferiors as "a lower form of animal life and none of the rules apply."[22] As in Poisonville, the rapacity of the rich is only the tip of the iceberg: everyone is on the take, even the purportedly objective newspapers. The publisher in *Red Harvest* pursued the truth, but Howard Mathews of the *Observer* toadies up to the bank that holds his mortgage and to bootlegger Shad O'Rory. Hammett underlines the failure of journalism as a moral force by juxtaposing a civic-spirited editorial with a scene in which gangsters tell Mathews what to print. The police are corrupt, of course, and District Attorney Farr is a political sycophant, prosecuting only those out of power, suppressing or refusing to investigate evidence that leads to the truth. The political system is beyond repair; Senator Henry not only raids the public treasury but murders his own son without trepidation. Even the private eye, Hammett's last just man, cannot combat this decay. When Beaumont tries to hire a detective to investigate his boss, Paul Madvig, the man refuses:"Fred and I are building up a nice little private detective business here. . . . A couple of years more and we'll be sitting pretty. I like you, Beaumont, but not enough to monkey with the man who runs the city" (*GK,* 172).

The hero of *The Glass Key* is thus not a private eye but a political lieutenant named Ned Beaumont. Physically he resembles his creator; he is tall, lean, wears a mustache; he is a compulsive gambler at cards, dice, and horses; he is a hard drinker, suffers from tuberculosis, and is cynical and tough.

The action begins when Ned Beaumont finds the corpse of Taylor Henry, the senator's son; he takes this information to his boss, Paul Madvig, owner of the East State Construction and Contracting Company and the local political boss, who urges Beaumont to do what he can to suppress a district attorney's investigation that is sure to follow. Madvig backs the senator and wants to marry his daughter Janet. Beaumont tells Madvig he ought "to sink" the senator, but out of loyalty he keeps District Attorney Farr from proceeding.

After a tangential episode in which he goes to New York City to collect a $3,250 gambling debt, Beaumont returns to find that someone has sent anonymous letters to everyone intimate with the crime. Each contains three questions, all of which imply that Paul Madvig killed Taylor Henry. The author appears to be Opal, Paul's daughter and Taylor Henry's paramour, but Beaumont prevents any official inquiry into this matter as well.

Then Madvig's political clubhouse begins to splinter; the dividing wedge is a foot soldier named Walter Ivans, whose brother Madvig refuses to spring from jail. Ivans takes his problem to Shad O'Rory, who eliminates witnesses to the offense. When Madvig declares war on O'Rory, Beaumont objects and there is a fistfight between the two. Then O'Rory offers Beaumont $10,000 to expose Madvig in the *Observer*. In an ensuing argument, Beaumont is knocked out, wakes up in a dingy room, and is beaten every day by two of O'Rory's thugs until he escapes.

In the hospital Beaumont tells a contrite Madvig and Janet Henry how he had planned to lay a trap for O'Rory: he then struggles out of the hospital to stop the *Observer* fom publishing the exposé to which he has inadvertently contributed. To do so he must confront O'Rory and Mathews at a cottage where they are holding Opal. Beaumont's rebukes and his seduction of the publisher's wife cause Mathews' suicide, but stop the publication.

After dinner at the Henrys', Beaumont interviews Janet about the murder. He discovers that the senator knew about the death before he himself found the body; he learns also that Janet is the author of the mysterious letters. Then a character named Sloss turns up with a clue, and suddenly all the evidence points to Paul Madvig. When Beaumont confronts him, Madvig makes an obviously false confession of guilt: he cannot account for Taylor Henry's hat, a clue that Beaumont chases throughout the plot. This impasse and their rivalry for Janet lead to the second rift between the two men.

Beaumont enlists Janet's aid only when they both vow to respect the truth that their collaboration turns up. Janet solves the hat trick, and Ned eliminates the threat from Jeff, a bad guy who strangles Shad O'Rory. There is nothing to do then but confront the senator with the evidence that he killed his own son.

The senator wants to commit suicide, but Beaumont refuses him the option and turns him over to the police. "He got mad at the thought of his son interfering with his chances of being re-elected and hit him," explains Beaumont to Janet Henry. Something like mutual respect affects them, and after they inform a stoic Madvig, the pair depart for New York City.

The character of Ned Beaumont

Critics of *The Glass Key* are troubled by the character of Ned Beaumont and the "tough guy" world in which he lives, for it is difficult to uncover in either any evidence that redeems him as a human being. Beaumont is so much more cynical than Sam Spade that his motivations are unclear. He seems to exist to take punishment. Robert Edenbaum points out that the reason Beaumont takes the beating from Jeff is never clear, and that "the mask is never lifted" so that the reader can discover Beaumont's feelings. Ben Ray Redman sees only sadism and heroic drinking in Beaumont, and Philip Durham calls him close "to being an amoral character." William Kenney's comment that *The Glass Key* is "Hammett's most ambitious study of moral ambiguity," however, leads to a more productive analysis.[23]

Hammett's "ambition" consists in working the realist vein without granting his protagonist the allegorical status usually given the detective: he limits Beaumont's effectiveness in the real world. Hammett strips him of the ability to move through all social strata, of physical prowess, pinpoint markmanship, and abductive powers. Beaumont is merely an "expediter" in a corrupt political machine: all that remains of the God-like in him is a vision of how things really are, which he will express to anyone who respects truth. Lacking the ability to make things happen, to author his and the other characters' destinies, Hammett's hero must focus on his own luck, for only that will help him escape the "falling beam." In other words, Hammett tailored Beaumont to meet the 1930s, an era in which that popular vision of idealism and action common to the 1920s (and represented by the Op) could no longer be sustained. An economic bubble had burst, and with it the illusion that there were falcons to seek.

Hammett introduced his hero as a man on a losing streak. Only a year earlier, Beaumont says, Paul Madvig "picked me up out of the gutter." But he is already losing again in his gambling, only "not so long—only a month or six weeks" this time. Economic hard times reduce the world to essentials; men make "low growling noises" in their chests, and the fellow next to Beaumont seems "hawk-nosed . . . a predatory animal of forty or so." To survive, Beaumont adapts. He becomes capable of planting evidence, protecting the guilty, manipulating the law, faking alibis, and approving of Madvig's graft, because he no longer has the illusion that he stands apart from the social organism. Its diseases are his diseases; it should not surprise readers that he hates "with a dull glow that came from far beneath the surface" of his eyes (*GK,* 95, 5, 31, 83).

In this Hobbesian universe, survival can be influenced by reason and ability but it is mostly the result of luck: either the beam falls or it doesn't. When luck is bad, Beaumont says, you "might as well take your punishment and get it over with." A change in luck is what sets in motion the plot of *The Glass Key.* Beaumont wins a big bet, his bookie skips town, and he decides to hunt him down. As he explains to Madvig, "it would be the same if it was five bucks. I go two months without winning a bet and that

gets me down. What good am I if my luck's gone? Then I cop, or think I
do, and I'm all right again. I can take my tail out from between my legs
and feel that I'm a person again and not just something that's being kicked
around" (*GK*, 5, 23).

Beaumont gets his money from the bookie by threatening to frame him
for the murder of Taylor Henry, a tactic unreproved by the author. This is
not what counts. By taking what is his, the protagonist reverses his luck:
"Ned Beaumont leaving the train that had brought him back from New
York was a clear-eyed erect tall man. . . . In color and line his face was
hale. His stride was long and elastic. He went nimbly up the stairs" (*GK*,
46).

The only trace of the private eye's pure power that remains in Beaumont
is his ability to see the world stripped of the overlays of civility, legitimacy,
and romance that blind others to its random and predatory nature.
Beaumont is a private *eye,* whose vision is his sole remaining quality of
allegoric status. He lives in a "large room in the old manner, light of
ceiling and wide of window, with a tremendous mirror." When the reader
first encounters him at home, "his feet rested in a parallelogram of late
morning sun" (*GK*, 16). The age of the room connotes authenticity of
vision, the emphasis on the mirror, windows, and light the actual
mechanics of vision, about which Hammett had been reading.
Throughout *The Glass Key* Beaumont is able to read the eyes of other men,
and Hammett reveals Beaumont's own inner state by describing his eyes.

It is because Beaumont sees the world with preternatural clarity that
Hammett must present scenes of shocking, seemingly gratuitous brutality. These were a staple of the tough-guy genre, of course, but they would
seem extraneous if Beaumont's vision of the world did not unite them. The
point is that, contrary to the fiction of the twenties, life is mostly
punishment for a good number of people. When Beaumont attempts
suicide rather than face continued beatings by Jeff, most critics assume
that simple sadism is operating, or that the hero fails to adhere to his tough
guy ethos, rather than seeing that Beaumont's collapse demythologizes
brutality.

Ned Beaumont was driven back against the wall. The back of his head struck
the wall first, then his body crashed flat against the wall, and he slid down the
wall to the floor. Rosy-cheeked Rusty, still holding his cards at the table, said
gloomily, but without emotion: "Jesus, Jeff, you'll croak him."
Jeff said: "Him?" He indicated the man at his feet by kicking him not
especially hard on the thigh. "You can't croak him. He's tough. He's a tough

baby. He likes this." He bent down, grasped one of the unconscious man's lapels in each hand, and dragged him to his knees. "Don't you like it baby?" he asked and, holding Ned Beaumont up on his knees with one hand, struck his face with the other fist.

Of the tough-guy character Joyce Carol Oates wrote "It is as if the world extends no further than the radius of one's desire." When the unprotected fall within that radius, they suffer. The victim has no good choices; he can only hope to get it over, and to move on, as Beaumont does when the bookie's bodyguard delivers a punishing body-blow: "He went down the stairs, loose-jointed, pallid and bare-headed. He went through the downstairs dining-room to the street and out to the curb, where he vomited. When he had vomited, he went to a taxicab that stood a dozen feet away, climbed into it, and gave the driver an address in Greenwich Village" (*GK*, 84, 32). The tough-guy world represents the diminished possibility of the heroic code in this world. The reader sensed that it took a great struggle for Sam Spade to decide that adherence to the code that kept him whole was more important than love, but the intent to survive is the only noble possibility in Beaumont's world.

The universality of this ethos highlights male behavior by reducing it. The way in which men behave toward one another has been a subject implicit in Hammett's work since *Red Harvest*. The Continental Op's male world consisted of inferiors and superiors, and few of the latter. Men existed in stratified relationships of clear authority; it was a chain of command world that mirrored the companies for which the men worked. Through most of *The Dain Curse* the same outlook prevailed, but in Quesada the Op dealt with an unranked circle of police and politicians to catch the murderer. The probing and mutual suspicion among them became the dominant male outlook in *The Maltese Falcon*. Spade's wariness, however, was directed at such flat characters as Gutman and Cairo, and only tentatively explored in his animosity toward Dundy and friendship with Polhaus. By the time of *The Glass Key*, Hammett had matured sufficiently as a creator of male characters to explore the relationship of one man to his best friend.

Male Friendships

Leslie Fielder has called it the classic American literary friendship: Jim and Huck, Chingachgook and Natty Bumppo, the affection of a Noble Savage and a Faust Without Sin. Paul Madvig and Ned Beaumont move

through a landscape as perverse as any created by Mark Twain, trying to
retain not innocence, for that has long vanished, but a minimum of
personal integrity. In stressing his sheer physical strength, his animal
characteristics, Hammett makes it clear that Paul is a kind of primitive.
Paul could not succeed without Ned, who sees the essential natures of
things. Like Huck, Ned seems to be without past, an orphan cut off from
"society" by a stigma, in this case his gambling. Only together are they an
effective unit, but the respect of each for the other's ability has come to an
end. "You don't talk to me like that . . . ," says Beaumont when Madvig
dismisses his vision, knowing that he, in turn, is denying Paul's power.

There are two fights between Beaumont and Madvig, and the novel's
conflicts and subplots are magnetized around them. After the first argument, in which Beaumont tells Madvig that he has been "outsmarted" by
the senator, there is a predictable fistfight and a peace that Hammett
describes with tough guy affection:

Madvig spoke hoarsely from deep down in him. "Ned."
Ned Beaumont halted. His face became paler. He did not turn around.
Madvig said: "You crazy son of a bitch."
Then Beaumont turned around slowly.
Madvig put out an open hand and pushed Ned Beaumont's face sidewise,
shoving him off balance so he had to put a foot out quickly to that side and put a
hand on one of the chairs at the table.
Madvig said: "I ought to knock hell out of you."
Ned Beaumont grinned sheepishly and sat down on the chair he had
staggered against. Madvig sat down facing him and knocked on the top of the
table with his seidel.
The bar-tender opened the door and put his head in.
"More beer," Madvig said. (GK, 71–72)

The second argument occurs after Madvig makes the false confession to
Taylor Henry's murder. Ned's ire is more explicable when readers understand that Madvig is tampering with the reality that informs Beaumont's
vision. When his most trusted confidant lies, Beaumont, a "fixer," is
bereft of his ability to repair reality. He cannot solve the mystery then
without Janet Henry, whose power as a senator's daughter and a quester
after truth are an aid, but do not make her a satisfactory substitute for
Paul.

Madvig does not appear again until Ned and Janet have laid Taylor's
murder at the senator's feet. Then Madvig appears at Beaumont's apartment to apologize and to square accounts, an intent that he carries out even
when Beaumont announces that Janet is leaving with him.

Madvig's lips parted. He looked dumbly at Ned Beaumont and as he looked the blood went out of his face again. When his face was quite bloodless he mumbled something of which only the word "luck" could be understood, turned clumsily around, went to the door, opened it, and went out, leaving it open behind him.

Janet Henry looked at Ned Beaumont. He stared fixedly at the door. (*GK,* 204)

Janet is the onlooker because the central relationship of the novel is between the two men, and its demise gapes at the reader as vacantly as the empty doorway. As the world grows more complex, deceptive, and unreadable, Huck and Jim grow rare. A breach can be forgiven once, but a breach reopened is a pattern, and in Hammett's world no one stands in the path of falling beams.

Beaumont and Janet Henry

A first reading of *The Glass Key* can leave the impression that the Ned–Janet liaison, which simmers for two thirds of the novel and boils only in the finale, is of paramount importance. The novel's title, after all, comes from an exchange between the two. Each had a dream about the other. Beaumont's is short. "I was fishing," he said, "and I caught an enormous fish—a rainbow trout, but enormous—and you said you wanted to look at it and you picked it up and threw it back in the water before I could stop you" (*GK,* 169).

It is a good dream for literary purposes, illustrating the Hammett hero's continuing distrust of women. The Continental Op trusted neither Dinah Brand nor Gabrielle Leggett, but gradually he grew more sympathetic, until in *The Maltese Falcon* Spade became most involved with the woman who most deceived him. In his incarnation as Beaumont, the hero has isolated himself from women. There is a version of Dinah Brand, named Lee Wilshire, who is scheming, attractive, and tough, but who fails to move Beaumont. He could seduce a flapper named Fedink, but he goes into the bathroom and is sick instead. Courtship itself has vanished; when Opal asks, "Aren't we friends?" Beaumont's reply is that "it's hard to remember it when we're lying to each other." (*GK,* 26) This points to a new female ideal; besides emotional toughness and a poker player's ability to bluff, the heroine needs a fierce respect for the truth:

Janet Henry leaned forward in her chair. "Why don't you like me?" she asked Ned Beaumont.

"I think maybe I do," he said.

She shook her head. "You don't. I know it."

"You can't go by my manners," he told her. "They're always pretty bad."

"You don't like me," she insisted, not answering his smile, "and I want you to."

He was modest. "Why?" (GK, 95)

Janet hides her emotions so effectively that Ned does not know, until a nurse tells him, that "she went out of here as near crying as anybody could without crying." But of course she *does not* cry, and Beaumont must shatter that dispassionate mask before he can allow her access to his emotions. Only when he succeeds, accusing her of being a Judith (an allusion to the biblical character who saved her people by killing her king), can Beaumont join forces with her. As he reduces her, Beaumont is "talking happily—not to her—though now and then he leaned his head over his shoulder to smile at her." She sits trembling, blanched, and silent, her femininity evident but checked by the masculine animus that attracts Beaumont. This encounter prompts the discussion of dreams. Janet's dream is much longer, and in the first telling she changes the ending.

we were lost in a forest, you and I, tired and starving. We walked and walked till we came to a little house and we knocked on the door, but nobody answered. We tried the door. It was locked. Then we peeped through a window and inside we could see a great big table piled high with all imaginable kinds of food. But we couldn't get in through either of the windows because they had iron bars over them.

This locale is important, for Bruno Bettleheim has attested: "Since ancient times the near impenetrable forest in which we get lost has symbolized the dark, hidden, near-impenetrable world of our unconscious. If we have lost the framework which gave structure to our past life and must now find our own way to become ourselves, and have entered this wilderness with an as yet undeveloped personality, when we succeed in finding our way out we shall emerge with a much more highly developed humanity."[24] Janet's dream continues:

Then we thought that sometimes people left their keys under door-mats and we looked and there it was. But when we opened the door we saw hundreds and hundreds of snakes on the floor where we hadn't been able to see them through the window and they all came sliding and slithering towards us. We slammed the door shut and locked it and stood there frightened to death listening to them hissing and knocking their heads against the inside of the door. Then you said that perhaps if we opened the door and hid from the snakes they'd come out and go away, so we did. . . . Then we jumped down and ran inside and locked the door and ate and ate and I woke sitting up in bed clapping my hands and laughing. (*GK,* 169–70)

In the novel's final scene, however, Janet adds, "I didn't tell you—the key was glass and shattered in our hands just as we got the door open, because the lock was stiff and we had to force it. . . . We couldn't lock the snakes in and they came out all over us and I woke up screaming" (*GK,* 202).

Janet's dream interprets the action of the novel, and indicates the diminished though realistic state in which Hammett leaves male-female relations. The house Janet dreams about represents the structure that she needs, the food the security of that structure. In actuality the only "key" that Ned and Janet find can unite them is a ruthless stripping away of each other's manners, illusions, and pretensions. A Freudian would say the snakes represent a male threat, and in fact this illusionless tough-guy milieu is an antifeminine world. Janet has a deep-seated, justifiable fear of life with Beaumont. When she lies about the ending of the dream, she flatters Beaumont by implying that he can put the lid back on Pandora's Box. But the dream reveals that the evil loosed cannot be vanquished. Beaumont's charges that she was a "whore" and her father a "pimp" are the *coup de grâce* in their mutual savaging. Their affection, like the glass key, "was stiff and we had to force it." The novel ends on a note of alienation as bleak as any canvas of Edward Munch. Janet watches Ned watch an empty doorway; she can only impersonate Sancho Panza to a visionary for whom quests are no longer possible. Instead of a house, they find the woods without end.

Criticism of *The Glass Key*

"Because it is not allegorical Gothic romance, lacking as it does a God-like Spade or Op, *The Glass Key* is Hammett's least satisfactory novel," writes Edenbaum.[25] Such a view, of course, limits Hammett's work to a genre, rather than recognizing his development as a complete writer. Seen in the progression of his work, *The Glass Key* is one of Hammett's best novels. He holds reader interest firmly while breaking free of the generic expectations that hounded him. He creates male relationships that are not merely hierarchical, and he elaborates a complex, pessimistic view of love.

Seen as a conventional novel, however, *The Glass Key* has its difficulties. There is fuzziness around the motives of the characters. "The question remains whether Paul was right in the first place, whether Ned acted out of desire for the girl rather than loyalty to Paul . . . ," Edenbaum concludes. But perhaps this is a strength. The question can be answered outside the generic limits implicit in this critic's judgment, if readers dare to see that Beaumont has been looking out for himself all along. Hammett gives liberal clues that this is just the case. Unfortunately, few readers see how fallen the hero is. The two principal lines of plot are set in motion by Beaumont's perception that you do not get what you want if you are willing to be trumped. He sees early that Shad O'Rory will overturn Madvig's empire because Madvig is unwilling to make free use of intimidation and murder. "That the hole Shad's put you in—or don't you think he'd go that far to put you in a hole?" asks Beaumont. (*GK,* 60) Madvig's idealistic refusal to fix a jail term becomes his weakness in an opportunistic, vicious world. Nor is man at love different from man at war. When Beaumont is in the hospital, he uses his injuries to attract Janet's attention, sizing up his opportunities behind "a tight, secretive smile." When Madvig solicits advice on appropriate presents, on proper attire, Beaumont knows the field is his if he wants Janet. And when Madvig tells him to "kiss off," he telephones Janet and invites her over, "whistling tunelessly under his breath." He pours himself a drink, puts on a fresh collar and starts a fire in the fireplace. When he tells Janet that Madvig killed Taylor, which he knows to be a lie, Beaumont is simply acting as a survivor. This is Poisonville, the corruption the Op sensed would make him "blood simple" has spread throughout the social organism, and the Hammett hero is free of the illusion that he stands apart.

Chapter Five

Lillian and *The Thin Man*

Fame

Hammett and his girlfriend Nell Martin left San Francisco in the fall of 1929 for New York City, where they expected to enjoy the publicity that city offers successful young writers. When Hammett rented a big apartment at 155 East 30th Street, the stock market had not yet crashed. Gossip columnists began to mention him, and his distinct appearance made him easily recognized in restaurants. But the new novel did not meet deadline. In February 1930, Hammett vowed to get it "finished somehow by the latter part of the next week." He completed *The Glass Key* in one continuous writing session of thirty hours, he said later, thereby ruining himself as a novelist. This may be apocryphal, but certainly Hammett was spending his energies carelessly.[1]

The publication of *The Glass Key* shortly after *The Maltese Falcon* brought Hammett to the attention of New York's most stylish tastemakers. Dorothy Parker "discovered" him for the *New Yorker,* though her praise had a bite that introduced Hammett to the vicissitudes of fame. She noted that his new hero, Beaumont, was

a man given perhaps a shade too much to stroking his moustache with a thumbnail, [who] can in no way stack up against the magnificent Spade, with whom, after reading "The Maltese Falcon," I went mooning about in a daze of love such as I had not known for any character in literature since I encountered Sir Launcelot. . . . I thought that in "The Glass Key" Mr. Hammett seemed a little weary, a little short of spontaneous, a little dogged about his simplicity of style, a little determined to make startling the ordering of his brief sentences, a little concerned with having his conclusion approach the toughness of the superb last scene of "The Maltese Falcon."[2]

Reviewers in San Francisco, when they took note of Hammett, had not endeavored to show their own stylistic superiority.

Hammett became caught up in New York's concern with style. He had a gift for repartee, and his new book review column in the *New York Evening Post* became more about Dashiell Hammett than he had permitted his earlier reviews to be. He had no patience now with his inferiors: "There is not much nourishment for adult readers in this group [of novels]. The first part of the Crawley work is acceptable melodrama, but the rest of it deals with rather aimless doings in African jungles. The other members of our list are, from beginnings to endings, carelessly manufactured improbabilities having more than their share of those blunders which earn detective stories as a whole the sneers of the captious."[3]

Later he claimed that he pushed most of the review books out of the way to get at the more attractively titled and jacketed ones. It is clear that Hammett helped to boost his own stock, but such self-promotion was not unique. Indeed, beside the campaigns of Pound and Hemingway, Hammett's efforts were modest. But he was successful; by the beginning of the summer he was no longer reviewing books. He had been snapped up by Hollywood as a screenwriter.

Warner Brothers had bought the screen rights to *Red Harvest* for $8,500 in 1929. Nothing happened until February 1930, when the studio released a completely rewritten version called "Roadhouse Nights."[4] The new treatment had little connection with Hammett's novel, but his credit line in the film increased his celebrity. At the age of thirty-six he was positioned to ask for what he wanted. Negotiating with David O. Selznick for a job at Paramount, Hammett built up his fame and bluffed the talent scout. "I believe that he is another Van Dine," Selznick reported to his boss, B. P. Schulberg, "indeed that he possesses more originality than Van Dine. . . . Hammett is unspoiled as to money, but on the other hand anxious not to tie himself up with a long-term contract. I was in hopes that we could get him for about $400 weekly, but he claims that is only about half of his present earning capacity between books and magazine stories, and I am inclined to believe him inasmuch as his vogue is on the rise."[5]

Hammett was hired. What happened to Nell Martin, to whom Hammett dedicated *The Glass Key,* is unknown, but Hammett moved to Hollywood. He was assigned to write an original story, which he did over a weekend. His script, "After School," consisted of seven handwritten legal-size pages. It required some rewriting, and the movie was credited to "Oliver H. P. Garrett from an adaptation by Max Marcin of Dashiell Hammett's original story." Thereafter Hammett worked regularly on scripts for Paramount's stars, including "Ladies' Man," a later Van Dine comedy that starred William Powell as the detective Philo Vance.[6]

Hammett now entered the stratified, opulent world of film society. His New York acquaintances, including Dorothy Parker and her husband Alan Campbell, moved to Los Angeles to write scripts. His circle included Herbert Asbury, Laura and S. J. Perelman, Arthur Kober, and his wife Lillian Hellman. As scriptwriters, none of them were among Hollywood's elite: they ranked below owners, producers, directors, and stars, all of whom made more money. But they could look down on minor actors, agents, cinematographers, and the various craftsmen needed to produce a motion picture. Most people in Hammett's circle seem to have been interested in moving up the scale. Having come to Hollywood for the good things that motion pictures promised, they lived as ostentatiously as possible, confident that soon they would be elevated to the wealth they saw on display.

Hammett took a nice apartment and hired as his chauffeur a black man named Jones. Numerous starlets, eager to meet the famous mystery writer, provided Hammett with a situation of which he took advantage. According to his biographer's research in the Veterans' Administration records, Hammett incurred his second case of gonorrhea in 1930. Some of the starlets did not appreciate Hammett's assumptions of their easy virtue. Court records show that Elise De Vianne sued him for rape, claiming he had invited her to dinner, beat her, and attempted intercourse. She asked $35,000 in damages, and was awarded $2,500 in a trial that Hammett did not attend.[7]

But Arthur Kober's wife was different. Kober was a screenwriter and a drinking buddy of Hammett's, later to become a well-known humorist. His wife, Lillian Hellman, worked as a script reader at M.G.M., and had been a copy editor at Boni and Liveright as well as a book reviewer for the *New York Herald Tribune*. "When I first met Dash," she wrote, "he had written the four novels and was the hottest thing in Hollywood and New York. . . . It was of interest to those who collect people that the ex-detective who had bad cuts on his legs and an indentation in his head from being scrappy with criminals was gentle in manner, well educated, elegant to look at, born of early settlers, was eccentric, witty, and spent so much money on women that they would have liked him even if he had been none of the good things."

Hammett spent his money rapidly—the good things were expensive. He began to drink more, and complained of headaches and deteriorating health until a script assignment from Warner Brothers pulled him out of the tailspin. He was asked to write an original Sam Spade story for William Powell. Hammett wrote "On the Make," later released as "Mister Dynamite," and he collected $10,000. He celebrated.

"On the night we had first met," reported Lillian Hellman, "he was getting over a five day drunk. . . . I was twenty-four years old and he was thirty-six. The five day drunk had left the wonderful face looking rumpled, and the very tall thin figure was tired and sagged. We talked of T. S. Eliot, although I no longer remember what we said, and then went and sat in his car and talked at each other until it was daylight. We were to meet again a few weeks later and, after that, on and sometimes off again for the rest of his life and thirty years of mine."[8]

Hammett wanted to live well. But with only a $1,000 advance on his next novel, he needed to exploit his reputation in New York. The depression caught up with him. According to Hellman, who went back with him, they were "very broke" when they took an apartment at 133 East 38th Street in May 1931. Hammett started a draft of *The Thin Man,* then put it aside to return to Los Angeles, one of several transcontinental shuttles that he and Hellman made at the time. Living "well" led to a midnight departure from the lavish Hotel Pierre; then, said Hellman, "He moved to what was jokingly called the Diplomat's Suite in a hotel run by our friend Nathanael West. It was a new hotel, but Pep West and the Depression had managed to run it down immediately." There Hammett read proof for *Miss Lonelyhearts* and met West's friend William Faulkner, who visited from Mississippi. "The three of us would meet each night," wrote Hellman, "sometimes early in the evening, sometimes very late, usually at Dash's place, arguing about books and drinking through until morning, when I would fall asleep or pass out, and they would eat breakfast or start another bottle."[9]

According to Faulkner's biographer, the drinking was nonstop. On one occasion Hammett and Faulkner pressed Bennett Cerf for an invitation to a dinner at Alfred Knopf's house, where Willa Cather was to dine. Cerf reluctantly made the arrangements, but when he picked up the pair at "21", he found they had been drinking since noon. Hammett subsequently passed out at the Knopf's dinner table.

They usually argued as they drank, frequently about Faulkner's *Sanctuary,* which the author disclaimed as a potboiler. The term "potboiler" bothered Hammett, who admired Faulkner and apparently felt that his own work, all within a popular genre, was condemned by implication. "Nobody ever deliberately wrote a pot-boiler," Hammett answered; "you just did the best you could and woke up to find it was good or no good." Usually, said Hellman, "they were both too drunk to listen to each other and each would speak at the same time."[10]

The food at the Sutton Club could be charged, and Hellman and West enjoyed reading the guests' mail, but life at a hotel for transients was depressing. Hammett wanted to make money and leave. He took up the fragment of *The Thin Man* and began to work on it. "Life changed," wrote Hellman, "the drinking stopped, the parties were over. The locking in time had come and nothing was allowed to disturb it until the book was finished. I had never seen anybody work that way; the care for every word, the pride in the neatness of the typed page itself, the refusal for ten days or two weeks to go out even for a walk for fear something would be lost."[11]

The Thin Man

For a reader progressing chronologically through Hammett's work, *The Thin Man* seems like a reprise. In this last novel, he neither extends his technical range nor deepens his thematic concerns. But he weaves a familiar fabric of characters, motifs, and situations that he hems with an overwhelming concern for style and irony.

This was not the case with Hammett's first version of *The Thin Man*, written in May 1931. The detective in the surviving original fragment is John Guild, the policeman in the later novel. He is sent by Detective Bureaus Inc. to investigate the claim of a client bank that a check belonging to Clyde Wynant has been altered from $1,000 to $10,000. Wynant is an eccentric writer similar in appearance to Hammett; the detective's search for him leads him into a murder case, and Wynant, like Owen Fitzstephan, appears to be the one guilty. Guild then becomes romantically involved with the victim's sister, who recalls Brigid O'Shaughnessy, when the fragment ends.

As it was rewritten, the high energy relationship of Nick and Nora Charles structures and redeems *The Thin Man*, although without disguising the recapitulations. The action is interrupted, as Peter Wolfe noted, with a set piece (the Alfred Packer tale). It has a debutante drawn to gangsters ("The Gatewood Caper" and "$106,000 Blood Money"), whose concern about a family curse and incest stem from Gabrielle Leggett. Nora, whose spunk and affection for detection owe something to Effie Perrine, seems to have inherited the wealth into which Gabrielle married.

Hammett returns to the first-person point of view, but he uses its inherent limits to keep the reader in the dark about information that

Nick Charles possesses, a technique Hammett deplored in other writers. The novel is set almost entirely in apartments and interiors, and its engines recur to classic detection formulas. The murder of Julia Wolf begins as a locked room problem; the inoperable gun and missing book are false clues, and the gathering of characters for the finale is a staple of English detection. The hero of *The Thin Man* reflects Hammett's changed circumstances. Nick Charles is an ex-detective who devotes some time to his wife's lumber mill and railroad fortune, the remainder to having a good time. No longer semi-allegoric, the detective must be drawn into the case by the curiosity of a vivacious woman, Nora, and his own past connections to the principals.

As the novel opens, Nick is drinking in a New York speakeasy when a beautiful young woman introduces herself as Dorothy Wynant, daughter of Clyde Wynant, an inventor for whom Nick had worked. She and her mother Mimi, who has divorced Wynant and married Christian Jorgenson, have come to New York to try to find Wynant. Nick suggests that Dorothy call Herbert Macaulay, Wynant's lawyer and an old Army buddy whose life Nick once saved. Later Nick learns from Macaulay that Wynant had dropped out of sight to work on a new invention, which looks suspicious when Julia Wolf, his secretary and paramour, is found murdered the next day. Wynant tries to prove his innocence through communiqués to Mimi, Dorothy, his son Gilbert, Macaulay, and even Nick Charles.

Since no Wynant likes any other family member, each attempts to manipulate information about the death. Nick can keep Mimi, with whom he had a liaison formerly, at arm's length; her lies are pathological and obvious. He is less successful with Dorothy, whose girlhood crush has matured into infatuation. She manages to accompany Nick and Nora home and to insinuate herself into her personal lives unnervingly. Gilbert is a precocious teenager who idolizes Nick and seeks the answers to odd questions, which Nick parries by referring him to the story of Alfred Packer in *Duke's Celebrated Criminal Cases*. Like the dream sequence in *Red Harvest* and the Flitcraft parable in *The Maltese Falcon,* this set piece holds a prominent position, but its thematic importance is slight.

The action accelerates after Shep Morelli bursts into the Charles' suite and mistakenly wounds Nick. Then Dorothy arrives, claiming that her mother beats her, and Gilbert announces that Dorothy is using his morphine. "I've been pushed around too much," Nick says. "I've got to see about things." Nick and Nora talk to and get leads from a heterogeneous cast: Harrison Quinn, a lecherous stockbroker who pursues Dorothy; his cynical wife Alice; Studsy Burke, owner of a speakeasy called the Pigiron Club; Morelli, an ex-con with cocaine nerves and a code of honor; Arthur Nunheim, another of Hammett's undersized stoolies; his girl friend Miriam; her boy friend, the blimpish Sparrow; and Levi Oscant (Oscar Levant, whom Hammet met at George S. Kaufman's home). For some readers, the most charming character is Asta, the Charles' schnauzer.

The mystery of Julia Wolf's death remains unsolved for some time; Wynant, Mimi, several underworld figures, Christian Jorgenson, and even Macaulay seem possible suspects. Nick must sort and compare the alleged messages from and appearances by Wynant to find the mastermind. When the stoolie, Numheim, is killed, his suspicions narrow. Wynant is either a fiction, or absent from the scene—someone is impersonating him. Then Wynant's body turns up.

Gathering the cast together, Nick points his finger at Macaulay. The lawyer must have killed Wynant months ago, he explains, and buried the body with the conflicting accoutrements in case of a slipup. Originally he had been defrauding Macaulay with Julia Wolf to cover his stock market losses with Quinn, but when Julia learned of Wynant's death, Macaulay could not trust her. She died too. Only Macaulay ever got phone calls from Wynant. His last possible escape was to have another eyewitness; he convinced Mimi to say she had seen Wynant. In return Macaulay said that he would cut her in on the inventor's estate without his knowledge. Nick Charles points out that if Wynant is dead, Mimi's children are his heirs. The estate is all theirs. "What do you want me to do . . . put him in cellophane for you?" says Charles, as he turns to the police.[12]

This terseness and masculine energy typify Charles only in the last part of the novel. In the preceding pages he is a talker, unlike the Op, and a prodigious drinker (twenty-nine drinks in ten days) who uses his retirement from detective work as an excuse for his disinterest in any quests. Peter Wolfe has written that in *The Thin Man* Hammett still "portrays the sleuth as a God figure," that "Nick saves Macaulay's life in the trenches and then takes it away after discovering the lawyer's guilt." Wolfe sees allegoric impulse in Charles's conversation: he calls the detective a "brilliant talker" who "controls conversations in which two subjects are being discussed at once."[13] But this is overstating the obvious—that Charles is facile at repartee—and understating the importance of action in allegoric communication. Nick is noticeably disconnected from the reality that grounded the philosophies and unraveled the mysteries of Hammett's earlier detectives. He does no legwork; the clues come to him. He engages in no fisticuffs, carries no gun; at his most violent, he punches his wife and throws a pillow at a gunman. This retreat from the physical world is necessary to sustain the irony and detachment that typify *The Thin Man,* but as the balance tips away from "reality" as the organizing principle of life, Hammett's detective becomes a creature of alienation rather than one driven by an ancient fever.

Nora is more satisfying, though she may seem to modern readers too much under Nick's finger. That she was one of the wittiest women in the fiction of the era owes to her model. Lillian Hellman, said Hammett, was the inspiration for the character. "I used to nag him to go back to work as a detective—chiefly so, in my mind, I could follow him around and see what would happen," the playwright said in 1969. "He'd grow very angry at the idea. But it also gave him something to write about."[14]

Nick and Nora Charles

The artistic core of the novel is the relationship between Nick and Nora. Long after the specifics of the murders have faded, readers remember the wit and tension that characterizes their marriage. Like Nick Carraway and Jordan Baker, or Jake Barnes and Lady Brett, Nick and Nora are in love and in competition at the same time; they are more nearly equals than any couple in American fiction since those of Kate Chopin. The popularity of psychology had prepared the public for the Charleses, but they are also products of the "sexual freedom" of the 1920s. Nora is the happy culmination of a long artistic evolution on Hammett's part. In early work he dealt only in female stereotypes, but his female characters increased in complexity until, in Janet Henry of *The Glass Key,* he found a woman tough enough to suit his disenchanted detective. The archetypal attraction of the hero for the succubus is transmuted into a sustaining interpersonal tension. Affection means that fights are now alliance-building, as the most artfully crafted parts of the novel show:

Nora sighed. "I wish you were sober enough to talk to." She leaned over to take a sip of my drink. "I'll give you your Christmas present now if you'll give me mine."

I shook my head. "At breakfast."

"But it's Christmas now."

"Breakfast."

"Whatever you're giving me," she said, "I hope I don't like it."

"You'll have to keep them anyway, because the man at the Aquarium said he positively wouldn't take them back. He said they'd already bitten the tails off the—"

"It wouldn't hurt you any to find out if you can help her would it? She's got so much confidence in you, Nicky."

"Everybody trusts Greeks."

"Please."

"You just want to poke your nose into things that—"

"I meant to ask you: did his wife know the Wolf girl was his mistress?"

"I don't know. She didn't like her."

"What's the wife like?"

"I don't know—a woman."

"Good-looking?"

"Used to be very."

"She old?"

"Forty, forty-two. Cut it out, Nora. You don't want any part of it. Let the Charleses stick to the Charleses' troubles and the Wynants stick to the Wynants'." (*TM*, 14)

One of the novel's triumphs is the way in which this marital tension is sustained; the closing lines, in which Nora responds to Nick's solution of the murder, "That may be . . . but it's all pretty unsatisfactory," indicate that for Hammett romance had become a state of improvised and shifting tension.

Hammett must have intended the Wynant clan to contrast with the Charleses, but the holiday atmosphere and ironic tone obscure the differences. This is unfortunate; the Wynants only appear to be dilettantes, when they should appear emotionally stunted or to embody a threat to the Charleses, in the way that the Leggett family might have. Only sporadically do the Wynants reveal their real natures. Mimi Wynant Jorgenson is obsessed with money, and can tell Nick Charles, "If you want Dorry, take her, but don't get sentimental about it." Dorothy is in some ways more terrifying. Raised in the new sexual freedom, she is unembarrassed about inserting herself into the Charleses' marriage. In his tone Hammett indicates a precociousness to this misplaced Electra Complex, but he also states that, looking at her, Nick Charles thinks "the result was satisfactory." For Dorothy, sex is a kind of consumption, with the attendant status and fleeting uniqueness. Her brother Gilbert, initially an appealing high school genius, reveals himself to be a peeping tom with incest fantasies. But the flatness of the Wynant curse (because these afflictions must seem amusing to harmonize with the overall tone) robs them of any chance to threaten Nick and Nora Charles.

This preoccupation with urbanity diffuses the novel's most ready source of tension. Such mordant sexuality, Hammett intimates, masks a greed that consumes "that portion around the breast." The story of Alfred Packer's cannibalism, an actual incident of Colorado history, indicates the underlying mechanics of the Wynant family. The thematic intent has been clear since George Thompson recognized that "what we see in the Wynant-Jorgenson family, the Quinn family, the Edge family, and the Nunheim family is cannibalism masquerading behind the illusion of the family compact. In each case, the motivation for their vicious behavior is a combination of greed and feeling of the necessity of self-survival, precisely the ingredients of the Packer story."[15]

Unfortunately, the counterpoint of theme and irony creates confusion, because the novel tends to parlor comedy rather than black humor. Many scholars have found the Packer incident expendable. They cite Lillian Hellman's interview with *Writer's Digest* in 1970, in which she said that Hammett used the Packer story simply to fill out a few pages. Richard Layman buttresses this view with a note that Nick's answers to Gilbert's questions about detective work, a few pages later, are lifted straight from Hammett's 7 June 1930 book review in the *New York Post.*[16]

The theme might have risen from the sexual tensions that structure so many of the novel's scenes: the interplay between Nick and Mimi, who talks about her "beautiful white body"; between Nick and Dorothy; between Dorothy and her stepfather; and between Dorothy and Gilbert. There are the broken marriages of the Quinns, Jorgensons, Nunheims, and Wynants. Liaisons predominate: Wynant and Julia Wolf, Quinn and Dorothy, Sparrow and Miriam, or Nora and Larry Crowley. Nick's estimate of the Wynant family—"They're all sex crazy"—applies to the whole population of the novel. Unfortunately, sexual mores are not handled with subtlety; rather they exist to serve the tone of cleverness. This was daringly avant garde in the thirties, though today it seems needlessly crude for Harrison Quinn to ask to touch the knee that Dorothy has straddled, or for Nora to assume that sex is "just business" for another woman. It establishes a base, however, for such urbanities as Alice Quinn's "What do people think about my staying with Harrison with him chasing everything that's hot and hollow?" The greatest flap centered, however, on this passage:

> "Tell me something, Nick. Tell me the truth; when you were wrestling with Mimi, didn't you have an erection?"
> "Oh, a little."

She laughed and got up from the floor. "If you aren't a disgusting old lecher," she said. (*TM*, 133)

Before serializing the novel, *Redbook* censored that passage, and some printings still use "excited" in place of "an erection." Hammett's publisher used the controversy to promote the novel, according to Layman. Alfred Knopf took out an ad in the *New York Times* that said, "I don't believe that the question on page 192 of Dashiell Hammett's *The Thin Man* has had the slightest influence upon the sale of the book. . . . Twenty thousand people don't buy a book within three weeks to read a five word question."[17]

The contrast between the worlds of the gangsters and of the Charles could also have contributed to the theme of greed and cannibalism, but Hammett compromised the truth that he knew about the underworld. The Pigiron Club becomes a nice place, where the Charleses slum for quaint ex-convicts, where they are protected from drunks by colorful bootleggers, and where Shep Morelli apologizes for shooting Nick. There is no contrast between the criminal and middle classes; as ways of life they are stained equally by lies, hypocrisy, and venality. But Hammett was not the painter of that tableau; his friends West and Fitzgerald were, and perhaps it was better left to them.

Technique in *The Thin Man*

The Thin Man has two climaxes. In the second, required by the English convention of the genre within which the book mostly falls, Nick explains the complexities of the case, for several pages, to an inquiring Watson named Nora. The first climax is the sort to which Hammett brought his Op stories. It prefaces the denouement and concerns truth and justice, the core of the detective's quest. This occurs when Nora asks if Macaulay is guilty beyond doubt, and Nick responds:

That's for juries, not detectives. You find the guy you think did the murder and you slam him in the can and let everybody know you think he's guilty and put his picture all over newspapers, and the District Attorney builds up the best theory he can on what information you've got and meanwhile you pick up additional details here and there, and people who recognize his picture in the paper—as well as people who'd think he was innocent if you hadn't arrested him—come in and tell you things about him and presently you've got him sitting on the electric chair. (*TM*, 174)

When Nora argues that his solution is "just a theory," Charles responds cavalierly, "Call it any name you like. It's good enough for me." So ends the weighing of the conflicting claims of justice, reality, and society; after five novels, a resolution that gets the plot finished is "good enough" for Hammett. The ennui explicit in this dismissal is more understandable if Hammett is understood to be describing his world, as it seems he was. What value could reside in writing about, or for, a world in which people are cannibals? In which the justice system is capricious? It is a state of meaninglessness too dire and unfocused to impel the creation of a fictional world. Unfortunately, Hammett would one day face precisely the juggernaut that he had imagined for Maucaulay.

Hammett endowed *The Thin Man* with proven technical flourishes. By this point, he knew what he did well. He was famous for his dialogue, his terseness, his toughness, and his irony. He gives readers all of these in *The Thin Man,* but he actually moves in a much narrower technical range. There are no new departures. He even forsakes the use of parataxis and hypotaxis, a tool of suspense writing, and writes much more uniform sentences, which average nineteen words in length (sentences in the early work average thirteen words). Screenwriting may have had something to do with the change; the cadence of Nick Charles's speech seems particularly fitted to delivery by a William Powell, as though Hammett were writing with a screenplay in mind. "It is the beginning of the end," he said later, "when you discover you have style."[18]

Irony was a hallmark that Hammett's public had come to expect. But his irony is no longer the result of cleanly juxtaposed events or unexpectedly appropriate responses; it becomes the ground of all social intercourse. Nick and Nora Charles can be ironic about anything, and it is almost a relief when guileless John Guild asks his straightforward questions. This irony has been appreciated by *The Thin Man*'s audience partially for its fidelity to a national conception of the era. By setting his novel in December 1932, the worst point of the Great Depression, Hammett tapped a powerful fantasy: that some people live unaffected by unemployment, inflation, bank failures, bankruptcy, and market collapses. The vague living the Charleses make off the remaining industrial skeleton is free of anxiety, and permits them self-indulgence. The setting seems, as Wolfe notes, in debt to Phillip Barry's play *Holiday,* which features the same gay New York holiday setting, witty repartee, and rich characters.

The few signs of his personal politics that Hammett left in the text are fragmented. His portrait of stockbroker Harrison Quinn, who loses

Macaulay's money, curdles in Quinn's alcoholism rather than in the parody of stock manipulations. "Those wild men from the West are going to give us some kind of inflation as soon as Congress meets," Quinn tells Charles, "and even if they don't, everybody expects them to." More wistful, because closer to Hammett's heart, is policeman Guild's plan to escape New York and set up a silver fox farm in the West. It is clear that, among the forces destabilizing society, Hammett regards "Communism" as a red herring. Nick Charles overhears a man saying, "Comes the revolution and we'll all be lined up against the wall—first thing." From his tone of voice, Charles concludes that the man thinks it is a good idea, but he goes away unperturbed. Aunt Alice Wynant is noted several times for her spinsterly insanity and fervid anti-Communism. "She's sure the Communists killed Julia Wolf," says Dorothy. "She thinks it's all over some secret they betrayed." Hammett's sentiments are those of the inventor Wynant, disowned by Aunt Alice because "he gave an interview to one of the papers saying he didn't think the Russian Five Year Plan was necessarily doomed to failure" (*TM*, 57).

For Hammett such perceived threats have nothing to do with the pathology of society. Prohibition, due to end the month after the action of the novel, has corrupted respect for law and faith in traditional values far more. In fact, everyone seems anxious to secure his full measure of illegal alcohol before it becomes legal and less exciting. The paradigm of the national condition is Macaulay, the lawyer turned murderer. He is a war buddy of Nick Charles, who saved his life in the trenches of Europe. Their relationship, forged on a primal experience, bonds them in society after the war. But less than ten years later the bond is meaningless, a ruse used by some men to manipulate others. A more damning portrait than a nation's betrayal of its own unifying experiences is difficult to imagine.

The novel was not an immediate best-seller, but according to Layman, "Hammett was able to live off the characters he created in *The Thin Man* for a long time." The book sold 34,000 copies at two dollars each in the first eighteen months—a lively market. Adding the serial sales to *Redbook* and the movie rights, Layman figures that the gross of the novel, its characters, and its spinoffs reached one million dollars by 1950.

Given Hammett's fame, *The Thin Man* received numerous reviews. Most were favorable. Dorothy Parker liked it, and the *New York Herald Tribune* called it "a new hardboiled opus worthy to stand beside the best of his other works." In the *New Republic*, however, T. S. Matthews noticed impurities when he assayed the ore: "Perhaps because he has turned the trick so easily before that he is now getting a little tired of it, perhaps because we are beginning to notice that he sometimes repeats his effects, 'The Thin Man' seems a less excitingly fresh performance than, say, 'The Maltese Falcon.' It is still heads-and-shoulder above any other murder mystery story published since his last one."[19] But the novel got a good reception in England, where readers were charmed by the familiar devices of English detection. Peter Quennell wrote, "It has every right to consideration on its literary merits." And Julian Symons said in 1972 that it was "a continually charming and sparkling performance."[20]

Hammett himself was later in accord with the *Times Literary Supplement*, which wrote in 1934, "This American detective story is told largely in dialogue, of which the object is rather to amuse with the smart phrase than to advance the movement. In fact there is little movement in it, if we deduct what goes to the getting of drinks and the making of telephone calls." More damning is an unpublished letter from Hammett to Hellman, written as he worked on the *Thin Man* screenplays in 1937: "I should stop this and go to work on some changes in my charming fable of how Nick loved Nora and Nora loved Nick and everything was just one big laugh in the midst of other people's trials and tribulations. Maybe there are better writers in the world, but nobody ever invented a more insufferably smug pair of characters. They can't take that away from me, even for $40,000."[21]

Hollywood

In May 1931 Warner Brothers released the first version of *The Maltese Falcon,* starring Ricardo Cortez. Though it was not a hit, things began to break fast for Hammett again. His agent lined up an anthology of mystery stories, and Hammett wrote a number of stories capitalizing on the movie; two are explorations of his feeling for Hellman, and another meditates on his declining career as a writer.

Hammett and Hellman left New York when *The Thin Man* appeared. "We got drunk for a few weeks in Miami," Hellman wrote, "then moved on to a primitive fishing camp in the Keys where we stayed through the spring and summer, fishing every day, reading every night. It was a fine year: we found out that we got along best without people, in the country."[22]

Hellman was at work on *The Children's Hour,* and Hammett, once interested in the dramatic possibilities of his work, gave her his best criticism. "He felt that you didn't lie about writing and anybody who couldn't take hard words was about to be shrugged off, anyway," reported

Hellman: "He was a dedicated man about writing. Tough and generous." His attention became focused more and more on her writing; he had benefited from good editors early in his career, and he passed on the experience.

Money began to come too easily, and Hammett made no effort to earn or retain it. King Features signed him to write continuity for a new comic strip called Secret Agent X-9. It was an effortless job, for which he earned $500 a week, yet his disregard for deadlines got him fired in fifteen months. Hellman said that Hammett's attitude was the result of "never believing in any kind of permanence," but contemporary judges of talent put it down to excessive drinking. Louis B. Mayer told his moviemaking associates that it was impossible to work with Hammett—he advised them not to try. "It had been a year of heavy drinking for both of us," wrote Hellman.[23]

Toward Hospitalization

This last year of productive work was Hammett's most remunerative, earning him between $50,000 and $80,000. He and Hellman rented a house on Long Island and began "throwing around the money from *The Thin Man.*"[24] They drank, they entertained, and apparently they quarreled. Hellman decided to go to Europe to a drama festival, and Hammett, who disliked foreigners, objected. But finally he gave her the money to go.

The Thin Man paid off exponentially when the movie, starring William Powell and Myrna Loy, was released by M.G.M. in June 1934. Hammett was hired again, this time by M.G.M. at $2,000 a week. He left New York, took a penthouse apartment in the Beverly Wilshire for $2,000 a month, and began to drink with a higher class of folk—Clark Gable, Joan Crawford, and Edward G. Robinson. He complained of being badgered by starlets, and implied that his celebrity kept him from getting any work done. In fact, he wrote to Hellman, he had only been to the studio once in the preceding eight days. It took him over two months to produce the thirty-four pages of his next movie treatment. The producer asked for a new draft, and the terms of Hammett's contract were revised, though he still earned a minimum of $1,000 a week, and $1,750 a week when he wrote dialogue. After nine months, he produced a 115-page movie story called *After the Thin Man*.

In the next three years Hammett was fired several times. He failed to report for work; he failed to honor deadlines; he walked off the set when he was needed; and he was drunk. He was rehired every time, and the contract stayed in effect for three years. It was "a tribute to his personal charm as much as anything," writes Layman, noting that Hammett had a "growing reputation as not only an unreliable writer but an uncooperative one as well." *After the Thin Man* was finally released in the holiday season of 1936, but the screenplay was credited to Hammett's friends Albert Hackett and Frances Goodrich.[25]

By the mid-1930s six films had been made from Hammett's original scripts or adapted from his stories. The nation was in a depression, but Hammett moved from his penthouse into the former mansion of actor Harold Lloyd and traveled in a limousine driven by Jones, with whom he had visited San Francisco and Albert Samuels earlier. But there were fewer of the pleasant Hollywood evenings with old friends that had typified his first residence. He was above his old friends now. When Nathanael West came from New York to write *The Day of the Locust,* his novel about Hollywood, he asked Hammett to get him on at M.G.M. He "made me eat plenty of dirt," West reported: "when I tried to talk to him about Stromberg and a job, he made believe he didn't understand what I was saying and called out in a loud voice so that everyone could hear, 'I haven't any money to lend you now, but call me next week and I'll lend you some.'"[26]

As he drank more, Hammett left unpaid bills everywhere—$1,000 for limousines, $1,500 for liquor, $11,000 for the penthouse. Both the Internal Revenue Service and the California tax authorities began to investigate. For a while Hammett seems to have lost all perspective. When Hemingway came to town and threw highball glasses into Dorothy Parker's fireplace, Hammett announced that "Ernest has never been able to write a woman. He only puts them in books to admire him." A while later, in a bar, Hammett stopped conversation by announcing that he did not like Hemingway's "lectures." "Why don't you go back to bullying Fitzgerald," asked Hammett, "Too bad he doesn't know how good he is." All reports indicate that Hammett left the bar unmarked.[27]

A few months later his drinking overtook him; Hammett went to the private section of the Lenox Hill Hospital to recuperate for several weeks early in 1936. Blanche Knopf, who had given him his first break, wrote to him, enclosing books to read, and reminding him that he had promised to write another novel. The drying out was not a complete success, but Hammett made a major change of direction in his life.

Chapter Six
Politics, War, and Prison
Duty

What happened to Hammett in Lenox Hill Hospital—whether he had a sudden realization or a gradual change of heart—is not known. Certainly he recognized the decline of his creative ability; he had done no substantial writing since *The Thin Man,* three years earlier. The shift in his personality, however, is less explicable.

One of its teachers had told the generation that matured in the twenties, "You are all conservatives who think it the duty of your generation to be liberal." For Hammett it was just the opposite. He had been fighting "duty" ever since he had been thrust on the streets at fifteen to make a living for his family. He had been camouflaging a materialism close to Marxism since his early stories, in order to produce detective-knights who enforced traditional conservative American values. At a point when his contemporaries, such as Max Eastman and John Dos Passos, were beginning to move toward conservatism, Hammett moved the opposite way.

Personal factors must have played a great role. Hammett faced the loss of his health, of his creativity, of most of his friends. He was isolated personally by his irascibility and, above all, by his irresponsibility. While he espoused the ideal in his fiction, he had not resisted the debauchery that success permitted. He had shed all sense of "duty," leaving a wife and two children, as well as numerous lovers, to fend for themselves. He broke nearly every contract or agreement that he had signed. He left unpaid bills and debts everywhere, often counting on others to pay them. He manipulated friends and employers. Now even Hellman had left, upset by the drinking that she called "heavy and dangerous."

Once an exemplar of flamboyance, Hammett was now as disillusioned and broken as some of his characters; he needed to reestablish himself. He began to reread Marx in the hospital, he reported later. He found in the German social and economic philosopher a moral writer whose energy sprang from deep convictions about injustice and the inevitability of change. In groping to understand the 1930s Hammett rethought his early materialistic leanings. The first thing, the easiest thing to do was to give away the money that flowed without effort, the money that he had never earned. "Sitting in New York, it was easy enough to write a check," said Hellman. As he became more openly Marxist, that is what Hammett did. Within a few years, he was contributing $1,000 a month to the Communist party.[1]

This was possible because in 1937 the money came in a flood. M.G.M. paid $40,000 for all rights to the characters of *The Thin Man* except those for the radio serialization. The serial, sponsored by Old Gold cigarettes, paid Hammett $500 a week. He got a new contract from M.G.M. paying $5,000 for a story synopsis, another $10,000 for its acceptance, and an extra $20,000 for a complete screen story.

But money could not correct all wrongs. After living alone in poverty with his two children for a decade, Jose Hammett filed for divorce in Mexican court. She lived in Santa Monica, just a few miles up the coast from the Lloyd mansion. The divorce was recorded on 31 August 1937, but an American judge later declared it to be without force.[2]

The public still thought him a celebrity, but Hammett knew that it was over. At first he envisioned a life in politics, with Hellman as his protégé. He donated money and time to causes associated with the Spanish Civil War. His allegiance to the idea of a world-wide revolution based on Marxist principles led him, with other writers of the era, to endorse Stalin's purge of dissenters and "counterrevolutionaries" such as Trotsky, even to sign a statement declaring, "The measures taken by the Soviet Union to preserve and extend its gains and its strength . . . find their echoes here, where we are staking the future of the American people on the preservation of progressive democracy and the unification of our efforts to prevent the fascists from strangling the rights of the people."[3] This was Hammett's opinion of the "New Deal."

Hammett returned to Hollywood to become a leading figure in a screenwriter's organization and other groups concerned about the rise of fascism in Europe. Often composed of European immigrants who had fled repressive regimes, these groups shared an idealistic, democratic vision of socialism and Communism at odds with the modern orthodoxies. "Most certainly he was a Marxist," wrote Hellman. "He was often witty and biting sharp about the American Communist Party, but he was, in the end, loyal to them," she said. "Once, in an argument with me, he said that of course a great deal about Communism worried him and always had and that when he found something better he intended to change his opinions."[4]

Hammett worked tirelessly for the Screenwriters Guild, establishing guidelines for employment and attempting to standardize screen credits. Since his former employer, M.G.M., led the fight against the union, Hammett was in the front lines. He solicited funds from friends for whom he had tremendous respect, such as Fitzgerald. He spoke at Communist sponsored rallies, and his biographer concludes that by 1938 he was probably a member of the party, although he never advocated overthrow of the United States government.[5]

Hammett's political interests drew him back and forth between Hollywood and New York, where he was briefly involved with a newspaper called *PM*, and a magazine titled *Equality: A Monthly Journal to Defend Democratic Rights and Combat Anti-Semitism and Racism*. He was on hand when the film "Another Thin Man" was released in November 1939. His income from his previous work was now over $60,000 a year, and his name was known internationally.[6]

The Maltese Falcon on Film

In 1941 John Huston ensured Hammett's continuing celebrity when he made as his first movie *The Maltese Falcon*. Huston was a good screenwriter; he saw, as Hammett had suggested to Block in 1929, that little need be done with the novel to turn it into drama. He did not soften Spade's character, as previous directors had, but directed Humphrey Bogart to play him as cynically as Hammett had written him. This Spade remains the classic, and even influences interpretations of the novel. He is a loner, who uses simpler people, such as Effie Perrine; he does not want to be touched, and he is violently antihomosexual. He enjoys hitting Wilmer and humbling Cairo. Like his director, this Spade enjoys testing himself against people and situations.

Huston became celebrated for his astute casting, and *The Maltese Falcon* was his initial triumph. Beside Bogart as Spade, he enlisted Mary Astor as Brigid O'Shaughnessy, Sydney Greenstreet as Casper Gutman, Peter Lorre as Joel Cairo, Gladys George as Iva, Lee Patrick as Effie, and Elisha Cook as Wilmer. Ward Bond and Barton MacLane were the cops. According to film scholar Louis Giannetti, the rakish Huston surprised the industry with his planning and thoroughness: "Everything was worked out in advance as much as possible. He made drawings for every setup, complete with camera instructions and details for the *mise-en-scène*. The movie was completed in two months, at the relatively low cost of $300,000. It was a huge success, both with the public and the critics. James Agee, who was to become Huston's most ardent critical champion, called the film 'the best private-eye melodrama ever made,' a judgement many critics would be reluctant to dispute even to this day."[7]

The central strength of the film is Bogart, whose portrayal of Sam Spade, said Pauline Kael, was "an ambiguous mixture of avarice and honor, sexuality and fear." Kael noted that Huston, "by shooting the material from Spade's point of view, makes it possible for the audience to enjoy Spade's petty, sadistic victories and his sense of triumph as he proves he's tougher than anybody. Spade was left a romantic figure, though he's only a few steps away from the psychotic."[8]

There are some omissions from the movie—namely, the references to homosexuality, the scenes concerning Brigid's night at Spade's apartment, and Spade's strip-search of Brigid. But none of these affects the theme as much as Huston's change of the ending. The musical score (by Adolph Deutsch) swells to a crescendo when Spade says, "I won't because all of me wants to." The theme becomes romantic; and since Huston discards the morning-after encounter between Spade and Effie, the final focus is on the romantic liaison rather than the embittered greed.

Hammett meanwhile was moving away from his celebrity in the literary and Hollywood worlds. He made an effort to put distance between *that* Hammett and himself. He had readopted duty, and seems even to have sought a sort of penance, a personal discipline. The American entry into World War II provided him with his opportunity.

War

Hammett tried to join the Army several times. In 1941, when he was forty-seven, he was turned down because of his age. In 1942, the Army checked its records and found that his earlier tuberculosis was active. Later the same year, having evaded his medical history somehow, he was turned down because his teeth were rotten. It is an indication of the importance he placed on military service that he paid for the dental work himself, and was accepted as a forty-eight-year-old private late in 1942.

Hammett's friends, especially Hellman, knew he had no business going to war. They sent him socks, mittens, and other clothes; Margaret Kober mailed him cakes and cookies. Hammett wrote back that "In lieu of going to the hospital—which is full as usual—I duck away from my auto mechanics twice a day and trot over to the Infirmary for inhalations—a vague sort of medication out of which it is possible that some half-hearted sort of benefit may come."

The Army stationed Hammett at Fort Monmouth, New Jersey, about thirty miles south of New York City. He was assigned, he wrote to Hellman, to "revise, correct, rewrite, coordinate, de-shit and otherwise make sense of three divergent courses in what they humorously but solemnly call 'army organization.' " In another letter, he described himself as "locked up in an office most of the day writing and revising Lessons Plans under the supervision of a young southern Lieutenant who is more womanly than lady-like."[9]

The upbeat note expresses some relief. The Army provided Hammett with an opportunity: service was patriotic, it was a political statement, it removed him from the Los Angeles–New York circuit, and allowed him to practice the equalitarianism that he preached. He probably suspected that the structured environment, and the calm spaces it afforded, would allow him to compose a new Dashiell Hammett to meet the world.

Hammett arrived on Adak, in the Aleutian Islands, on 8 September 1943, having spent some time at Camp Shenango in Pennsylvania. Camp Shenango was a "containment center" for men whom the Army considered subversive; the plan was to keep Hammett and others there under close watch for the length of the war. But Eleanor Roosevelt learned of the plan, protested to the president and the men at Shenango were dispersed.

Hammett was sent to the Aleutians, an area that returned to its prehistoric peace after the Japanese were routed earlier in 1943. There was an unusually large group of Shenango men on Adak, many of whom felt it was simply another, colder form of stockade. Hammett described the scene:

The wind is blowing down the stovepipe, filling our hut with fumes of the diesel oil we burn. Another wind, I guess, is blowing up through the cracks between the floor and walls in my corner of the hut. Somehow it doesn't clear away the fumes, but it does chill my fingers and the coca-cola I keep under my bunk, showing there's some good and some bad in everything, except maybe the kind of Kay Kaiser program that our radio is re-broadcasting right now. . . .[10]

Brigadier General Harry Thompson was the commander on Adak. An admirer of Hammett's work, the general gave him a job to which he assigned top priority: starting a camp newspaper. Thompson wanted the men to be oriented and entertained, to feel that their efforts were part of an international effort. His sponsorship allowed Hammett an unusually free hand; he subscribed to the *Daily Worker,* which was delivered via camp mail, and he reread Marx again.

By 1945 Hammett was considering the renewal of his "serious" writing career. He wrote to Hellman that, though he had no clear idea, he felt a novel pressing its way out. He told another friend that he was considering a novel about a man who comes home from the war and does not like his family. In his letters, he put acquaintances on notice that he intended to pace his life differently when he returned.

I'm even thinking about maybe perhaps it might be possibly writing a novel, for which I've got a kind of feel if not exactly any very clear ideas. We'll see. It's kind of hard to convince me that I haven't all the time in the world ahead of me for practically anything I wish to do. It's a nice feeling even if it may when analyzed turn out to be just sheer shiftlessness. Maybe Alaska's got something to do with it.[11]

He spent his last half year of service, as he had begun, writing army training manuals. Stationed at Fort Richardson, outside Anchorage, he drank more and complained about sitting at a desk all day. On 27 June 1945 he was promoted to master sergeant, and on 6 September he was discharged. "I'm the only one who ever really saw it," he said later. "The footing was poor, and the GIs walked with their heads down, afraid of slipping. I looked up, and saw such mountains and lakes as no other place can match."[12]

Prison

Before Hammett went to war, Hellman bought a 130 acre estate in New York's Westchester County. On his return, he looked forward to spending time there, but he was puzzled by Hellman's apparent coolness toward him. "I guess maybe you forgot you were going to write twice a week," he wrote to her, "or does that only start applying when I reach Capetown or Kamchatka?" Her seeming disregard made him wary.[13]

He took an apartment at 15 East 66th Street in New York and divided his time between there and Westchester at first. His royalties from the radio serializations netted $1,300 a week, according to Layman. During the day he read, ranging from Gore Vidal and Jack Kerouac to Marxist political treatises. In the afternoon, beginning in 1946, he taught classes in mystery writing at the Jefferson School of Social Science, a school dedicated to "Marxism as the philosophy and social science of the working class." Hammett thought his role was that of discussion leader, and once brought Frederic Dannay (of the pseudonymous Ellery Queen team) to critique the students' work.[14]

At Hellman's Hardscrabble Farm Hammett turned to scientific and factual reading, to the nature that he loved in the Aleutians. "This afternoon I was very much the nice old-man-puttering-around-in-suburbia," he wrote. "I planted some gloxinias and cut some sprays of forsythia for indoor forcing and put out fresh suet cakes and seed for the birds and was just too sweet for words all the way around. Maybe I can find a ladybird on the sturdy windowsill and kick it around to show I'm young and vigorous."[15]

Hammett's political activities continued. In 1946 he became president of the Civil Rights Congress of New York, a group cited as subversive by the attorney general. Even newspapers such as the *New York Journal American* began to comment on the prominence of his Communist associations. All totaled, said the *American,* Hammett was affiliated with thirty-six groups "named as Communist fronts by Congressional or State committees."[16]

In 1949, the Civil Rights Congress posted over $250,000 to free eleven men convicted of conspiracy to teach and advocate the overthrow of government by force. Four of the eleven failed to appear to begin their sentences. The court decided to ask the trustees of the bail fund where the men were: the position of Hammett and the other trustees was that such questions were irrelevant to locating the fugitives. As Richard Layman points out, it was impossible for Hammett *not* to know: "Minutes of the CRC bail fund meetings were kept and they were initialed by all the trustees, including Dashiell Hammett. . . . CRC documents subpoenaed by the court seem to indicate that Hammett's position was not merely honorary, that he actually had a major role in formulating the policy of the bail fund committee."[17]

There could be little doubt about the result of non-cooperation: Frederick Vanderbilt Field refused to testify before Hammett and was sentenced to six months. When Hammett took the stand on 9 July 1951 he refused to answer most questions. At the conclusion he was found guilty of contempt, put in custody until 7:30 P.M., and then sentenced to six months.

In late September he was transferred to the Federal Correctional Institute at Ashland, Kentucky, where he began to correspond with his daughter Josephine: "The mop handle felt kind of good in my hands this morning—Monday, Wednesday and Friday are mop days—and I realized

I'd been looking forward to it: I guess I was either feeling good or going crazy—or both." He served twenty-two of his twenty-six-week sentence; he got four weeks off for good behavior.[18]

Hammett had not paid any income tax since the twenties. While he was in prison the Internal Revenue Service caught up with him and audited his royalties. It assessed his liability through 1950 at $111,000, and attached all of his income to pay the debt. Not that there was much: pressure from the witch-hunters forced the networks to drop his serials, and publishers to let his books go out of print. Hollywood purged itself of "fellow travelers." Hammett could not have gotten anyone at a studio to answer his phone call, much less give him a scriptwriting job. In the five years after his release, his royalties were less than $5,000—and the I.R.S. collected them all.

Hellman's finances sagged similarly: she sold the Hardscrabble Farm to pay her bills, and moved back to New York City: Hammett moved into the gate-house of the Katonah, New York, estate of Dr. Samuel Rosen, an acquaintance who sympathized with his political views. "I did know from what he said about 'Tulip,' the unfinished novel," reported Hellman; "that he meant to start a new literary life and maybe didn't want the old work to get in the way. But sometimes I think he was just too ill to care, too worn out to listen to plans or to read contracts. The fact of breathing, just breathing, took up all the days and nights."[19] As the years went on Hammett became a hermit. "The ugly little country cottage grew uglier with books piled on every chair and no place to sit, the desk a foot high with unanswered mail," wrote Hellman. "The signs of sickness were all around."[20]

It was on such a figure that Senator Joseph McCarthy chose to vent his anger in 1953. He called Hammett before the Permanent Subcommittee Investigation of the Senate Committee on Government Operations, which was checking on the State Department's book buying policy for its overseas libraries. McCarthy wanted to make sure that no books by Communists went abroad. Since 300 copies of eighteen volumes of Hammett's work were in embassy libraries, he was an obvious target. Questioned first by Roy Cohn and then by McCarthy, Hammett talked more than he had at his earlier trial, but he took the Fifth Amendment and evaded direct answers to questions about his political views. When he failed to remember the particulars of his book publications, McCarthy asked such questions as "Have you ever engaged in sabotage?" His books were removed from the embassies, but replaced when President Eisenhower said that they posed no threat.[21]

"Tulip"

Hammett's last effort at fiction, "Tulip," was finished or abandoned in 1952–53, and published only in 1966. A character named Tulip visits Pop, who is trying to write a novel. Pop does not like his visitor and they argue about what sort of experience should be in the novel. The action moves slowly, searching for a way to tell a story without depending on a narrative line.

Few scholars have looked at "Tulip" seriously or aligned it with Hammett's earlier work. But, at least in its first part, "Tulip" is a carefully written story. Not only its descriptions of the countryside but many of its structural details are carefully crafted. Hammett never wrote a better transition, for example, than this one:

Tulip was usually longwinded—especially when he thought it necessary to back into one of his tales—but the guts of what he told me, not in his language and without any of the thoughts he said he had at the time, was that Lee Branch said, "The flag is waving," and lowered his head a little to peer up under his dun hat brim through cattail tips.[22]

What follows is a flashback neatly fitted to the tone of the first-person narrator.

"Tulip" is also a thoughtfully structured piece that continues many of Hammett's long-standing themes. It seems unrelated to Hammett's previous work only if readers forget where he left Ned Beaumont, the ragged hero of his last serious novel. At the novel's end Beaumont and Janet Henry are allied, the semblance of a family, faced with an open door. The traditional concerns with power, fame, money, have been outmoded; they will improvise a life. This is more or less the state in which the reader finds Pop, the narrator of "Tulip." He is stuck in the doorway between his cold, rational interior and Tulip, this character from his past, who delights in his fund of experience.

Tulip comes to convince Pop to listen to him and to write "his novel." He finds Pop beside a pond, where he has been hunting ducks; they talk and walk back to the house where Pop is visiting. They talk more after dinner, with drinks and cigars. Hammett allows both the narrator and Tulip to try out anecdotal styles, but apparently he is not satisfied with them.

Adhering to a pattern established in his first novel, Hammett places in the center of the story a lacuna—his own early review of a book on

Rosicrucianism. Tulip produces the review and makes fun of its pomposity. Unhappily, the narrator must agree—it is awful writing. But he asks if he can have a copy, "I'd forgotten it," he explains. He likes, but cannot defend, his early book review, introducing an ambiguity about his attitude toward his past. There are themes, an innocence perhaps, that he wishes to rediscover. There are other themes, illustrated by the anecdote about the plot of "The Girl with the Silver Eyes," which he wishes to forget. The counterpointed passages highlight Hammett's search for a mature style. For a few pages he progresses, but then he tires and serves up old anecdotes. Nothing emerges: there is no "new style." If anything, the unfamiliar reader will be more intrigued by the "old" style than by the search for a new one.

The other major struggle of "Tulip" is for a persona. Pop is a quietly cynical narrator, just released from prison, hounded by the I.R.S. He is rootless, rational, and skeptical. His only remaining value is his intellectual honesty, a refusal to lie about what he *knows*. But as the story proceeds, Hammett destroys this empathetic quality by not allowing the character to name his real needs—a family, a home, a substantial world in which to deploy his intellect.

Unfortunately it is his failure to define a new realm here, more than anything else, that dooms Pop in his struggle with his past. Natty Bumppo cannot *think down* the juggernaut of civilization. There are several promising conflicts in "Tulip"—Pop's instruction of Tony in the use of the deadly crossbow is one. But Pop does not know how to spread the field of possibilities before Tony; he is too caught up in the comfortable machismo of cigars, liquor, and anecdote.

Without a present realm, organization becomes a problem: there is no significant action, and Hammett does not make the thematic tension manifest. He tries to excuse the lack several times. "Almost is pretty good as a result," he says. But the progress is tortuous, bumping along tale by anecdote. An audience accumulates, mostly children, to listen. Will the new persona, Pop, defeat the incarnation of his past, Tulip?

I was floundering a little now. Talking through Tony had seemed to make things easier for me, as Tulip had probably known, but I hadn't been able to find the key to this new combination. I don't mean that Do and Lola were likely to be an unsympathetic audience. They weren't. They liked me, and jail had even given me glamor, but what I was talking about—or trying to talk about—hadn't anything to do with that. . . . So I went on, doing the best I could to tie them in along the way. (*T,* 342)

This struggle for a sense of audience is curious, until the reader remembers that originally Hammett's audience had been given to him, narrowly defined, by Cap. Shaw. He worked out of that conception his entire career. Now, seeking a more intelligent public, he guarded against the faults he perceived in the intellectuals he had been reading (Beckett, Sartre, Heine):

if you're careful enough in not committing yourself you can persuade different readers to see all sorts of different meanings in what you've written, since in the end almost anything can be symbolic of anything else, and I've read a lot of stuff of that sort and liked it, but it's not my way of writing and there's no use pretending it is. (*T,* 345)

Hammett had paced his cell, and measured its walls. No mode of storytelling satisfied him any more. Indeed he seemed at odds with the very idea of fiction, of unreality and its function and importance in life. "No feeling can be very strong if it has to be shielded from reason," says Pop.

There is little left but to frame the best possible speech of concession. Thinking of Tulip, Pop concludes:

I had a wary feeling that he might come to represent a side of me. His being a side of me was all right, of course, since everybody is in some degree an aspect of everybody else or how would anybody ever hope to understand anything about anybody else? But representations seemed to me—at least they seem now, and I suppose I must have had some inkling of the same opinion then, devices of the old and tired, or older and more tired—to ease up, like conscious symbolism, or graven images. If you are tired you ought to rest, I think, and not try to fool yourself and your customers with colored bubbles. (*T,* 352)

The story ends there. The view that "Tulip" is a fragment derives from the implicit application of a generic norm. In fact "Tulip" is a typically modernist exploration of a form for a personal end. Genres may be broken, altered, or discarded; what matters is that the quester arrive at something sufficient as personal truth. When Hammett found his he could not have been too surprised that it spelled the end of writing.

The Summing Up

Hammett measured his every breath after his time in prison. "I am concentrating on my health," he told an interviewer; "I am learning to be a hypochondriac." The tuberculosis that felled his mother had caught up with him. As in San Francisco, he could only sit up for short periods; when he complained of this, and of pains in his chest, Hellman took him to see a Park Avenue specialist.

The doctor told Hellman that it was cancer of the lungs and that it was inoperable, but she chose not to tell Hammett, though he was not long fooled. "He did not wish to die," she wrote,

and I like to think he didn't know he was dying. But I keep from myself even now the meaning of a night, very late, a short time before his death. I came into his room, and for the only time in the years I knew him there were tears in his eyes and the book was lying unread. I sat down beside him and waited a long time before I could say, "Do you want to talk about it?"

He said, almost with anger, "No. My only chance is not to talk about it."

And he never did. He had patience, courage, dignity in those last awful months.[23]

Hammett died on 10 January 1961, about two months later, in Lenox Hill Hospital. A veteran of two wars, he was buried at Arlington National Cemetery. At the funeral, which was not much noticed, Hellman delivered a eulogy calling him "a man of simple honor and great bravery."

Nor did much attention focus on the probate of his will, since it was known that the I.R.S. had liens of over $200,000 against Hammett for unpaid back taxes. He left half his estate to his daughter Josephine, one quarter to daughter Mary, and one quarter to Hellman, whom he named executrix. Two years later Hellman and Arthur Cowan began a series of complex legal manuevers, which are detailed thoroughly by Layman, aimed at acquiring the copyrights of the estate. Initially they offered the I.R.S. $2,000 to settle the $200,000 tax lien. This was rejected, but eventually the government accepted a settlement of $5,000. For the grand total of $6,786, Hellman and Cowan won rights to all of Hammett's copyrights, though whatever royalties had accrued since 1952 went to the government. Neither Hammett's daughters nor his estranged wife, to whom he was still married legally, were left with any claim on his work.

Since his death, Hammett's work has been in print continually. The five novels and two collections of short stories were published under the Vintage (Knopf) imprint in 1972, and have remained in print. Even *The Dain Curse,* Hammett's least popular novel, has sold over 70,000 copies since 1970. CBS television adapted the book for a three-part series in 1978 and paid a reported $250,000 for the rights.[24]

Hammett's rediscovery by the movies, of course, only confirms what his fellow writers knew in the twenties and thirties: there was a great dramatic center to his work. "The key scenes in Hammett," said Ellery Queen, "are not the spectacular bloodlettings, but the quiet, intense interplays of character in dialogue." A reviewer, Richard Schickel, saw later that "Hammett, a leftist, regarded moral evil as economically determined. . . ."

People who followed mystery writing closely—Frederic Dannay, Cap. Shaw, Raymond Chandler—were the first to tell the world exactly how good Hammett was. Then reviewers like Ben Ray Redman explained Hammett and Chandler—"the two modern greats"—to audiences in the *Saturday Review*. Clifton Fadiman would write that "the school of hard-boiled fiction . . . birthed two masters, [the first] being Dashiell Hammett."[25]

That his accomplishment broke out of the genre might have gone unrecognized had Hammett not written *The Maltese Falcon*. Though some critics argue for *The Glass Key*, and a few for *Red Harvest*, the *Falcon* is by most estimates Hammett's finest novel. "From it emerged a new kind of detective hero," said Ross Macdonald, "the classless, restless man of American democracy, who spoke the language of the street. . . . He possesses the virtues and follows the code of a frontier male. Thrust for his sins into the urban inferno, he pits his courage and cunning against its denizens, plays for the highest stakes available, love and money, and loses nearly everything in the end." Even his envious contemporary, Dorothy Parker, praised it: "He does his readers the infinite courtesy of allowing them to supply descriptions and analyses for themselves . . . he sets down only what his characters say, and what they do."[26]

The Maltese Falcon was read by Fitzgerald, Faulkner, and Hemingway. When Gertrude Stein came to the United States in 1934, Dashiell Hammett was the writer she wanted to meet. She took his work back to France; soon Andre Malraux called Hammett a link between realism and modernism, and Andre Gide would say, after reading *Red Harvest*, that it was "a remarkable achievement, the last word in atrocity, cynicism and horror." Hammett became the preferred fare of Somerset Maugham, who called him "an inventive and original writer," of whose characters "any novelist would have been proud to conceive." He was translated eventually into French, Spanish, Italian, and German, and has won the respect of modern writers as disparate as James Michener and John Hawkes.[27]

In the pantheon of mystery and detective writers, Hammett's place is near the head. Among American practitioners, only Edgar Allan Poe stands before him and only Raymond Chandler stands beside him. Hammett cleared the way for a generation of writers that included Macdonald, Spillane, Simeon, Le Carre, and the spy novelists, because he introduced into an effete, prescribed genre the vigor of the street, the tension of contemporary problems.

As an innovator of this magnitude, Hammett deserves consideration not only as a detective writer, though an understanding of his accomplishment is impossible without that framework, but also as a significant American novelist. He stands, as Malraux tried to argue, between the realism of Dreiser and Crane and the modernism of Hemingway and Pound. Though not the equal of these writers, he stands above James M. Cain, John O'Hara, or James T. Farrell. He had the ability, as major writers do, to break genres and make something new of them. As Ross Macdonald put it, "Hammett was the first American writer to use the detective-story for the purposes of a major novelist, to present a vision, blazing if disenchanted, of our lives." Said Chandler, "Hammett took murder out of the Venetian vase and dropped it into the alley; it doesn't have to stay there forever, but it looked like a good idea to get as far as possible from Emily Post's idea of how a well-bred debutante gnaws a chicken wing."[28]

As a stylist—a writer attended to by other writers—Hammett is even more important. Like Hemingway in prose, and William Carlos Williams in poetry, he focused attention on the American language. "He had style, but his audience didn't know it," wrote Chandler, "because it was in a language not supposed to be capable of such refinements. They thought they were getting a good, meaty melodrama written in the kind of lingo they imagined they spoke themselves. It was, in a sense, but it was much more. . . . He was spare, frugal, hard-boiled, but he did over and over again what only the best writers can ever do at all. He wrote scenes that seemed never to have been written before."[29]

Notes and References

Chapter One

1. Richard Layman, *Shadow Man, The Life of Dashiell Hammett* (New York, 1981), pp. 129–30. My respect for this book is great; it is *the* book on Hammett, and an exceptional piece of research and investigation accomplished in adverse conditions. New books by Diane Johnson and William Nolan were not yet available when the present volume went to press.
2. Ibid., p. 5.
3. William Nolan, *Dashiell Hammett, A Casebook* (Santa Barbara, Calif., 1969), p. 11.
4. Layman, *Shadow Man,* p. 7.
5. Ibid.
6. Lillian Hellman, *An Unfinished Woman, a Memoir* (New York, 1979), p. 238.
7. Layman, *Shadow Man,* p. 8.
8. Ibid.
9. Nolan, *Dashiell Hammett,* pp. 11–12.
10. Hellman, *An Unfinished Woman,* p. 271.
11. Dashiell Hammett, manuscript of "Seven Pages," at the Humanities Research Center, University of Texas–Austin (hereafter this location cited as HRC).
12. Dashiell Hammett, letter in *Black Mask* 7, no. 9 (November 1924):128.
13. Hammett, "The Hunter," HRC.
14. Layman, *Shadow Man,* p. 12.
15. Ibid.
16. Nolan, *Dashiell Hammett,* p. 12.
17. Hammett, "From the Memoirs of a Private Detective," *Smart Set* 70, no. 3 (March 1923):88–90.
18. Hellman, *An Unfinished Woman,* p. 227.
19. Nolan, *Dashiell Hammett,* p. 14.
20. Ibid., p. 16.
21. Hammett, "Seven Pages" and "Women Are a Lot of Fun, Too," HRC.
22. Herb Caen, quoted in Nolan, *Dashiell Hammett,* p. 56.
23. Layman, *Shadow Man,* p. 22.

24. Nolan, *Dashiell Hammett,* p. 18.
25. Hammett, "Seven Pages," HRC.
26. Layman, *Shadow Man,* p. 24.
27. Ibid., pp. 24–25.
28. Nolan, *Dashiell Hammett,* p. 18.
29. Ibid., p. 19.
30. Hellman, *An Unfinished Woman,* p. 232.
31. Layman, *Shadow Man,* p. 26.
32. Ibid., p. 27.
33. Hammett, "The Great Lovers," *Smart Set* 69, no. 3 (November 1922):4.
34. Layman, *Shadow Man,* p. 30.
35. Hammett, "Memoirs," pp. 89–90.

Chapter Two

1. William Ruehlmann, *Saint with a Gun: The Unlawful American Private Eye* (New York, 1974), p. 22.
2. Edgar Allan Poe, *The Collected Works of Edgar Allan Poe* (New York, 1965), 14:358.
3. Ibid., pp. 309, 33, 331, 360.
4. Ruehlmann, *Saint with a Gun,* pp. 26, 28, 29.
5. Henry Nash Smith, *The Frontier in American History* (New York: H. Holt & Co. 1920), p. 2.
6. Leslie Fiedler, *Love and Death in the American Novel* (New York, 1960), p. 476.
7. John Carroll Daly quoted in Philip Durham, "The Black Mask School," in *Tough Guy Writers of the Thirties,* ed. David Madden (Carbondale, Ill., 1968), pp. 56–57.
8. Steven Marcus, Introduction, to *The Continental Op,* by Dashiell Hammett (New York, 1975), p. xxi.
9. Hammett, "Nelson Redline," p. 3, HRC.
10. Hammett, "An Inch and a Half of Glory," HRC.
11. Hammett, "Faith," p. 10, HRC.
12. Ibid., pp. 1–2.
13. Hammett, "The Hunter," p. 61, HRC.
14. Ibid., beginning of manuscript unpaged.
15. Hammett, "Itchy," HRC.
16. Hammett, "The Tenth Clew," in *The Continental Op* p. 34; hereafter cited in the text as *CO.*
17. Hammett, *The Big Knockover* (New York, 1972), pp. 81, 91; hereafter cited in the text as *BK.*
18. Layman, *Shadow Man,* pp. 73–75.
19. Walker Gibson, *Tough, Sweet and Stuffy* (Bloomington, 1975), p. 41.

20. Hammett, "The Sign of the Potent Pills," HRC.

21. Raymond Chandler, *The Simple Art of Murder* (New York, 1972), pp. 16–17.

Chapter Three

1. Hammett to Blanche Knopf, 11 February 1928, HRC.

2. Blanche Knopf to Hammett, 12 March 1928, HRC.

3. Hammett to Blanche Knopf, 20 March 1928, HRC.

4. Hammett to Blanche Knopf, 9 April 1928, HRC.

5. Hammett, *Red Harvest* (New York, 1972), p. 4; hereafter cited in the text as *RH*.

6. Cited by Layman, *Shadow Man*, pp. 92–93.

7. Ibid., p. 96.

8. Maloney in Nolan, *Dashiell Hammett*, pp. 49–50.

9. Ibid., pp. 46, 48.

10. Hammett, *The Dain Curse* (New York, 1968), p. 90, p. 89; hereafter cited in the text as *DC*.

11. The critics are William Kenny, "The Dashiell Hammett Tradition and the Modern American Detective Novel" (Ph.D. dissertation, University of Michigan, 1964), p. 104; Layman, *Shadow Man*, p. 100; and George J. Thompson, "The Problem of Moral Vision in Dashiell Hammett's Detective Novels" (Ph.D. dissertation, University of Connecticut–Storrs, 1972), p. 52.

12. Hammett to Blanche Knopf, 20 March 1928, HRC.

13. Hammett, *The Dain Curse*, pp. 25, 35; Marcus' Introduction, p. xx.

14. Information on names from Layman, *Shadow Man*, p. 104; Hammett reaction, p. 70.

15. George Grella, "Murder and the Mean Streets: The Hard Boiled Detective Novel," in *Detective Fiction: Crime and Compromise*, ed. Dick Allen and David Chacko (New York, 1974), p. 423.

16. Layman, *Shadow Man*, p. 100.

17. For publication data see ibid., p. 104–5.

18. Ernest Hemingway, *Death in the Afternoon* (New York, Scribners, 1932), p. 228.

19. Hammett to Block, 16 May 1929, HRC.

20. John Martin, quoted by Nolan, *Dashiell Hammett*, p. 50.

Chapter Four

1. Hammett, Introduction to *The Maltese Falcon* (New York, 1934), p. vii.

2. For details, see Layman, *Shadow Man*, pp. 110–11.

3. Hammett, *The Maltese Falcon* (New York, 1972), p. 220; hereafter cited in the text as *MF*.

4. See Layman, *Shadow Man,* p. 112, and Paul Kress, "Justice, Proof and Plausibility in Conan Doyle and Dashiell Hammett," *Occasional Review* 7 (1977):121.

5. Bernard Schopen, "From Puzzles to People: the Development of the American Detective Novel," *Studies in American Fiction* 7, no. 2 (1979):180.

6. S. F. Bauer, L. Balter, and W. Hunt, "The Detective Film as Myth: The Maltese Falcon and Sam Spade," *American Imago* 35 (1978):282.

7. Grella, "Murder and the Mean Streets," p. 417.

8. Nolan, *Dashiell Hammett,* p. 58.

9. Ibid., p. 63.

10. Character information, ibid., p. 59.

11. Kenney, "The Dashiell Hammett Tradition," p. 110; Ross MacDonald, in Nolan, *Dashiell Hammett,* p. 63.

12. Thompson, "The Problem of Moral Vision," pp. 112, 115–16.

13. Nolan, *Dashiell Hammett,* p. 61.

14. Robert Edenbaum, "The Poetics of the Private-Eye: The Novels of Dashiell Hammett," in *Tough Guy Writers of the Thirties* (Carbondale, Ill., 1968), p. 82.

15. Hammett to Block, 16 June 1929, HRC.

16. Hammett to Block, 31 August 1929, HRC.

17. Shaw, quoted in Nolan, *Dashiell Hammett,* p. 57.

18. Reviews summarized by Layman, *Shadow Man,* pp. 112–13.

19. Hammett to Asbury, 6 February 1930, HRC. Chandler, *The Simple Art of Murder,* p. 17; Ross Macdonald in Nolan, *Dashiell Hammett,* p. 63.

20. Hammett to Knopf, 19 September 1929; Hammett to Asbury, 6 February 1930, HRC.

21. The citations in sequence: David T. Bazelon, *Commentary* 7 (May 1949):471; Robert Edenbaum, "Poetics of the Private Eye," p. 99; and Phillip Durham, "The Black Mask School," in *Tough Guy Writers,* p. 71.

22. Hammett, *The Glass Key* (New York, 1972), p. 9; hereafter cited in the text as *GK.*

23. Edenbaum, "Poetics," p. 102; Durham, "School," p. 70; Kenny, "Tradition," p. 93.

24. Bruno Bettleheim, *The Uses of Enchantment* ((New York: Vintage, 1977), p. 94.

25. Edenbaum, "Poetics," p. 100.

Chapter Five

1. Hammett to Block, 21 August 1929; Hammett to Asbury, 6 February 1930; Hammett to Hellman, 30 April 1931, HRC.

2. Dorothy Parker, *New Yorker,* 25 April 1931, p. 91.

3. Hammett, *New York Post,* 7 June 1930, p. 54.

4. Details from Layman, *Shadow Man,* p. 125.

5. Ibid., p. 126.
6. Ibid.
7. Ibid., p. 136.
8. Hellman, *An Unfinished Woman* pp. 228, 226.
9. Ibid., pp. 235, 154.
10. Joseph Blotner, *Faulkner: A Biography* (New York: Random House, 1975), pp. 741–42; Hellman, *Unfinished Woman,* p. 154.
11. Hellman, *Unfinished Woman,* p. 236.
12. Hammett, *The Thin Man* (New York, 1972), p. 171; hereafter cited in the text as *TM.*
13. Peter Wolfe, *Falling Beams: The Art of Dashiell Hammett* (Bowling Green, Ohio, 1980), p. 162.
14. Joyce Haber, "Lillian Hellman Takes a Look at Today's Theatre," *Los Angeles Times,* 2 November 1969, p. 15.
15. Thompson, "The Problem of Moral Vision," p. 182.
16. Layman, *Shadow Man,* p. 145.
17. Ibid.
18. Hammett, cited in ibid., p. 116.
19. Figures and critics cited in ibid., pp. 141, 147.
20. Cited by Wolfe, *Falling Beams,* p. 148.
21. Hammett to Hellman, 26 December 1937, HRC.
22. Hellman, *An Unfinished Woman,* p. 237.
23. Hellman, *Pentimento* (New York, 1973), pp. 171, 101, 74.
24. Ibid., p. 101.
25. Details from Layman, *Shadow Man,* pp. 159–60.
26. Cited by Jay Martin, *Nathanael West: The Art of His Life* (New York: Farrar, Straus & Giroux, 1970), p. 268.
27. Hellman, *An Unfinished Woman,* pp. 58–60.

Chapter Six

1. Hellman, *An Unfinished Woman,* p. 56; and Layman, *Shadow Man,* p. 183.
2. Layman, *Shadow Man,* p. 167.
3. Ibid., p. 173.
4. Hellman, *Unfinished Woman,* p. 230–31.
5. Layman, *Shadow Man,* p. 175.
6. Ibid., pp. 178–83.
7. Louis Giannetti, *Masters of American Cinema* (Englewood Cliffs, N.J.: Prentice Hall, 1981), p. 251.
8. Pauline Kael, *New Yorker,* 29 April 1981, p. 28.
9. Hammett to Margaret Kober, 16 November 1942, HRC. Second letter cited by Layman, *Shadow Man,* p. 187. Third letter by Hammett, n.d., file 1, letter 1, HRC.

10. Hammett, letter, 1943, HRC.

11. Conversation cited by Layman, *Shadow Man,* p. 198; letter of 4 March 1945, HRC.

12. Cited by Layman, *Shadow Man,* p. 199.

13. Hammett to Hellman, 15 June 1943, HRC.

14. Layman, *Shadow Man,* p. 212.

15. Hammett, letter, 24 February 1951, HRC.

16. Layman, *Shadow Man,* p. 211.

17. Ibid., p. 220; Hellman, *Unfinished Woman,* p. 228.

18. Hammett to Josephine Hammett Marshall, 3 November 1951, HRC.

19. Hellman, *Unfinished Woman,* p. 224.

20. Ibid., pp. 241–42.

21. Details in Layman, *Shadow Man,* pp. 228–30.

22. Dashiell Hammett, "Tulip," in *The Big Knockover* (New York, 1972), p. 311; hereafter cited in the text as *T.*

23. Hammett quoted in Layman, *Shadow Man,* p. 234; Hellman, *Unfinished Woman,* p. 225.

24. Details in Layman, *Shadow Man,* pp. 237–39.

25. Ellery Queen in *The Creeping Siamese,* by Dashiell Hammett (New York: Dell, 1950), p. 7; Schickel quoted by Nolan, *Dashiell Hammett,* p. 99; Redman and Fadiman, ibid., p. 121.

26. Ross MacDonald, "The Writer as Detective Hero," in *The Mystery Writer's Art* (Bowling Green, Ohio, 1970), p. 299; Dorothy Parker, "Oh Look! A Good Book!" in *Constant Reader* (New York: Viking, 1970), p. 135.

27. Malraux and Gide cited by Layman, *Shadow Man,* p. 164; Somerset Maugham, "The Decline and Fall of the Detective Story," in *Vagrant Pleasures* (Garden City, N.Y., 1953), p. 127.

28. Ross MacDonald, "The Writer as Detective Hero," p. 300; Raymond Chandler, "The Simple Art of Murder," in *The Simple Art of Murder,* p. 16.

29. Ibid., pp. 16–17.

Selected Bibliography

PRIMARY SOURCES

1. Novels
Red Harvest. New York and London: Knopf, 1929.
The Dain Curse. New York and London: Knopf, 1929.
The Maltese Falcon. New York and London: Knopf, 1930.
The Glass Key. New York and London: Knopf, 1931.
The Thin Man. New York: Knopf, 1934; London: Barker, 1934.

2. Story Collections
$106,000 Blood Money. New York: Spivak, 1943.
The Adventures of Sam Spade & Other Stories. New York: Spivak, 1944.
The Continental Op. New York: Spivak, 1945.
Hammett Homicides. Edited by Ellery Queen. New York: Spivak, 1946.
Dead Yellow Women. Edited by Ellery Queen. New York: Spivak, 1946.
Nightmare Town. Edited by Ellery Queen. New York: Spivak, 1948.
The Creeping Siamese. New York: Spivak, 1950.
Woman in the Dark. Edited by Ellery Queen. New York: Spivak, 1951.
A Man Named Thin. New York: Spivak, 1962.
The Big Knockover. Edited by Lillian Hellman. New York: Random House, 1966.
The Continental Op. Edited by Steven Marcus. New York: Random House, 1974.

3. Other Books
Creeps by Night. Edited, with an introduction, by Hammett. New York: John Day, 1931.
Secret Agent X-9. Books 1–2. Philadelphia: David McKay, 1934. A two-volume collection of Hammett's comic strip.
The Battle of the Aleutians. By Hammett and Robert Colodny. Adak, Alaska: Intelligence Section, Field Force Headquarters, Adak, 1944.

4. Manuscripts
The preponderance of Dashiell Hammett's manuscripts and letters are held by the Humanities Research Center, University of Texas at Austin. These materials

range from unpublished early stories to the Hellman-Hammett correspondence
to the galley proofs of *The Continental Op.*

SECONDARY SOURCES

1. Bibliography

Layman, Richard. *Dashiell Hammett, A Descriptive Bibliography.* Pittsburgh:
University of Pittsburgh Press, 1979. A thorough bibliography, with
reproductions of first edition dust jackets and bindings. An essential
research tool, also of interest to collectors.

2. Books

Cawelti, John. *Adventure, Mystery, Romance.* Chicago: University of Chicago
Press, 1976. Useful background.

Champigny, Robert. *What Will Have Happened.* Bloomington: Indiana University Press, 1977. Limited relevance to Hammett, but an interesting
theory of detective fiction as play.

Chandler, Raymond. *The Simple Art of Murder.* New York: Ballantine, 1972.
An important essay on American detective fiction that postulates Hammett as prime mover.

Fiedler, Leslie A. *Love and Death in the American Novel.* New York: Stein and
Day, 1966. Useful, provocative background.

Fletcher, Angus. *Allegory: The Theory of a Symbolic Mode.* Ithaca, N.Y.: Cornell
University Press, 1964. Long, detailed, historical study of allegory from
ancient through modern time.

Gibson, Walker. *Tough, Sweet & Stuffy.* Bloomington: Indiana University
Press, 1975. Useful discussion of modern American prose.

Haycraft, Howard. *Murder for Pleasure.* New York: Appleton-Century, 1941.
A section on Hammett and his contributions to the detective story.

Hellman, Lillian. *An Unfinished Woman.* New York: Bantam, 1979. An
exceptional piece of autobiography, with stories and anecdotes about
Hammett. Accuracy and chronology are questionable.

————. *Pentimento.* New York: Signet, 1973. Useful in same way as preceding.

Layman, Richard. *Shadow Man: The Life of Dashiell Hammett.* New York:
Harcourt Brace Jovanovich, 1981. *The* biography of Hammett. An extraordinary piece of research, presented with great objectivity. A book to
which this study owes much.

Madden, David, ed. *Tough Guy Writers of the Thirties.* Carbondale: Southern
Illinois University Press, 1968. Contains four good essays about Hammett, including the seminal piece by Edenbaum.

Maugham, Somerset. *The Vagrant Mood.* Garden City, N.Y.: Doubleday & Co., 1953. Contains an interesting essay on detective fiction that treats Hammett.

Nevins, Francis M., Jr. *The Mystery Writer's Art.* Bowling Green, Ohio: Bowling Green University Press, 1970. Important background, several of the same essays as in Madden, and an important essay by Ross MacDonald touching on Hammett.

Nolan, William F. *Dashiell Hammett: A Casebook.* Santa Barbara, Calif.: McNally & Loftin, 1969. The first book about Hammett's life and writing. A good gathering of information, very readable, but too admiring and undocumented. Biographical details superseded by Layman's work.

Pinkerton, Allan. *The Expressman and the Detective.* Chicago: W. B. Keene, Cooke, 1875.

Poe, Edgar Allan. *The Complete Works of Edgar Allan Poe.* Edited by James A. Harrison. 17 vols. New York: AMS Press, 1965.

Ruehlmann, William. *Saint with a Gun: The Unlawful American Private Eye.* New York: New York University Press, 1974. Well written, interesting study of historical background and contemporary morality of detective heros, with chapter on Hammett.

Sayers, Dorothy. *The Omnibus of Crime.* New York: Harcourt, Brace, 1929. Useful introduction to history of detective story.

Vidocq, Eugene-François. *Vidocq: The Personal Memoirs of the First Great Detective.* Translated and edited by Edwin Gile Rich. Cambridge, Mass.: Riverside Press, 1935. Useful historic background.

Wolfe, Peter. *Beams Falling: The Art of Dashiell Hammett.* Bowling Green, Ohio: Bowling Green University Press, 1980. First published full length study of the Hammett corpus. Some good insights and new information, but often facile and wandering.

3. Articles

Bauer, Bates and Hunt. "The Detective Film as Myth: *The Maltese Falcon* and Sam Spade." *American Imago* 35 (1978):275–96.

Blair, Walter. "Dashiell Hammett: Themes and Techniques." In *Essays in American Literature in Honor of Jay B. Hubbell.* Durham, N.C.: Duke University Press, 1967.

Burelbach, F. M. "Symbolic Naming in *The Maltese Falcon.*" *Literary Onomastic Studies* 6 (1979):226.

Durham, Philip. "The *Black Mask* School." In *Tough Guy Writers of the Thirties.* Carbondale: Southern Illinois University Press, 1968, pp. 51–79.

Edenbaum, Robert I. "The Poetics of the Private-Eye: The Novels of Dashiell Hammett." In *Tough Guy Writers of the Thirties,* pp. 80–103.

Grella, George. "Murder and the Mean Streets." *Contempora,* March 1970, pp. 8–20.

Gonzalez, C. G. "Hammett, Chandler, Hellman—el regréso de la serie negra." *Neuva Estafeta* 5 (1979): 111–13.

Kress, Paul. "Justice, Proof and Plausibility in Conan Doyle and Dashiell Hammett." *Occasional Review* 7 (1977): 208–14.

Malin, Irving. "Focus of *The Maltese Falcon:* The Metaphysical Falcon." In *Tough Guy Writers of the Thirties,* pp. 104–9.

Marcus, Steven. "Dashiell Hammett and the Continental Op." *Partisan Review* 41 (1975): 363.

Nolan, William F. "Shadowing the Continental Op." *Armchair Detective* 8 (1974): 121–32.

Sale, Roger. "Dashiell Hammett." *On Not Being Good Enough.* Oxford: Oxford University Press, 1979, pp. 73–80.

Schopen, Bernard. "From Puzzles to People: the Development of the American Detective Novel." *Studies in American Fiction* 7, no. 2 (1979): 175–89.

4. Dissertations

Kenney, William P. "The Dashiell Hammett Tradition and the Modern American Detective Novel." University of Michigan, 1964.

Parker, Robert Brown. "The Novels of Dashiell Hammett, Raymond Chandler, and Ross MacDonald." Boston University, 1971.

Thompson, George J. "The Problem of Moral Vision in Dashiell Hammett's Detective Novels." University of Connecticut–Storrs, 1972.

Index

DATE DUE

DEMCO 38-297